THE WORLD: SANCTUARY AND BATTLEFIELD

Reflections on Jesus' final prayer
in John 17

DANIEL BOURGUET

Foreword by Bob Ekblad

Translated from the French

THE PEOPLE'S SEMINARY PRESS

The following is a list of books by
DANIEL BOURGUET that have been published
in English translations

Repentance — Good News!
(La repentance, une bonne nouvelle)

Spiritual Maladies (Les maladies de la vie spirituelle)

Becoming a Disciple (Devenir disciple)

The Silence of God during the Passion
(Le silence de Dieu pendant la Passion)

Praying the Psalms (Prions les Psaumes)

From Darkness to Light (Des ténèbres à la lumière)

The Tenderness of God (La tendresse de Dieu)

Encounters with God (Rencontres avec Jésus)

The Humble Divinity of Jesus in Mark's Gospel vol 1
(L'humble divinité de Jésus dans l'évangile de Marc
Tome 1)

The Humble Divinity of Jesus in Mark's Gospel vol 2
(L'humble divinité de Jésus dans l'évangile de Marc
Tome 2)

On the banks of the Jordan (Sur les bords du Jourdain)

The last words of Jesus before the Cross
(Le dernier entretien avant la croix)

Philemon of Gaza meditates Mark's Gospel
(Le moine Philémon de Gaza médite l'Évangile de Marc)

Philemon of Gaza meditates Matthew's Gospel
(Le moine Philémon de Gaza médite l'Évangile
de Matthieu)

Happy are the pure in heart (Heureux les coeurs purs)

The first seven volumes listed above were published
by Cascade Books. The others in this present series are
published by The People's Seminary Press. For further
details, see www.danielbourguet.com

THE WORLD: SANCTUARY AND BATTLEFIELD

Reflections on Jesus' final prayer
in John 17

THE WORLD: SANCTUARY AND BATTLEFIELD
Reflections on Jesus' final prayer in John 17

The People's Seminary Press
Burlington, WA 98233
www.peoplesseminary.org
ISBN: 978-1-954387-18-8

Translated from the original French edition.
Daniel Bouguet, *Le monde, sanctuaire et champ de bataille,*
Lyon: Éditions Olivétan, 2002.
Copyright @ 2002 Éditions Olivétan, Lyon, France.

Bible passages are literal translations of the French. The author uses a range of French translations.

CONTENTS

TRANSLATOR'S NOTE

In these translations of Daniel Bourguet's books, we have generally added a short note such as this, making a few observations: for example, that an effort has been made to be gender inclusive where the French tends not to be. Translator's footnotes have been added since it is felt that this adds to the richness of the text; these notes have been endorsed by the author. Daniel does not speak English; however, we are in regular communication with him.

The title "The World: Sanctuary and Battlefield. Reflections on Jesus' final prayer in John 17" adds an explanatory subtitle to the original French, *Le monde, sanctuaire et champ de bataille*. The book complements "The last words of Jesus before the Cross," which examines John 14–16. RW

FOREWORD

THE PUBLICATION OF DANIEL BOURGUET'S BOOKS IN English is a valuable contribution to the literature of contemplative theology and spirituality that will nourish and inspire the faith of all who read them. Daniel Bourguet, a French Protestant pastor and theologian of the Huguenot tradition, lives as a monk in the mountainous Cévennes region in the south of France. There at his hermitage near Saint-Jean-du-Gard, Daniel maintains a daily rhythm of prayer, worship, Scripture reading, theological reflection, and spiritual accompaniment. All of his books flow out of a life steeped in love of God, Scripture, and the seekers who come to him for spiritual support.

I first met Daniel Bourguet in 1988 when my wife, Gracie, and I moved from rural Central America to study theology at the Institut Protestant de Théologie (IPT), where he taught Old Testament. The IPT is the Église Réformée de France's[1] denominational graduate school in Montpellier, France.

Prior to our move to France, while ministering among impoverished farmers in Honduras in the 1980s, we came across the writings of the Swiss theologian Wilhelm

1. Now Église Protestante Unie de France.

Vischer and the French theologian Daniel Lys by way of footnotes in Jacques Ellul's inspiring books. Vischer had written a three-volume work entitled *The Witness of the Old Testament to Christ*, of which only volume 1 is translated into English.[2] That book, along with a number of articles and Daniel Lys' brilliant *The Meaning of the Old Testament*,[3] exposed us to a community of Bible scholars who articulated a continuity between the Old and New Testaments that was highly relevant both then and now. This connection ultimately led me to Bourguet.

We experienced firsthand how a literal reading of the Old Testament in isolation from the New Testament confession that Jesus is both Lord and Christ (Messiah) brings great confusion, division, and even destruction. In rural Honduras churches often distinguish themselves by selectively observing Old Testament laws and using certain Old Testament stories to inspire fear of God as a punishing judge. North American Christians at this time were drawing from the Old Testament to justify the death penalty and US military intervention in Central America and beyond.

Wilhelm Vischer, an active resister of Nazism from his Old Testament teaching post inside Germany, resisted the misuse of Scripture to justify anti-Semitism, nationalism, and war, insisting on the importance of the Old Testament for Christian faith at a time when it was being dismissed. He was consequently one of the first professors of theology to be pressured to leave his post and eventually depart Nazi Germany before World War II. He served as Karl

2. Wilhelm Vischer, *The Witness of the Old Testament to Christ*, vol. 1, *The Pentateuch*, trans. A. B. Crabtree (London: Lutterworth, 1949).

3. Daniel Lys, *The Meaning of the Old Testament* (Nashville: Abingdon, 1967).

Barth's pastor in Basel after he, too, left Germany. After the war, the church in France, having been widely engaged in resistance to Nazism and deeply encouraged by Barth, invited Vischer to be the professor of Old Testament at the IPT in Montpellier.

The biblical reflections of Ellul, Vischer, Lys and other French theologians led Gracie and I to look into theological study in France.[4] We wrote the IPT about their graduate program and discovered that Vischer had long since retired after training several generations of pastors. His protégée, Daniel Lys, had recently retired but was still available. Lys's place had been filled by his doctoral student, Daniel Bourguet, who also had been trained by Vischer. The IPT welcomed us with a generous scholarship, and we soon made plans to learn French and move to Montpellier.

After being immersed in Bible studies with impoverished farmers in war-torn Honduras, we were eager for help in understanding Scripture. Disillusioned with America after being engaged in resisting US policy in Central America, we felt drawn to reflect from a different context. We reasoned that studying in a Protestant seminary with a history of persecution in a majority Catholic context would prove valuable. We left Tierra Nueva in the hands of local Honduran leaders and moved to Montpellier in July 1988 to study French and then began classes in September

Daniel Bourguet taught us Hebrew and Old Testament in ways that made the language and text come alive. He invited students into his passion and curiosity as we

4. We assumed there were others where these came from, and were able to study with pastor and New Testament professor Michel Bouttier, who was also trained by Vischer and published broadly, including a commentary on Ephesians and a number of collections of provocative articles. Elian Cuvillier followed Bouttier as Professor of New Testament at the IPT, writing many high quality books and articles.

pondered both familiar and difficult passages of Scripture. I remember continually being surprised at how seriously Daniel took every textual critical variant, even seemingly irrelevant ones. He masterfully invited and guided us to both scrutinize and contemplate each variant in its original language until we understood the angle from which ancient interpreters had viewed the text. Daniel modeled an honoring of distinct perspectives as we studied the history of interpretation of each passage. He sought to hold diverse perspectives together whenever possible, yet only embraced what the text actually permitted, exemplifying fine-tuned discernment that inspired us.

Daniel's thorough approach meant he would only take us through a chapter or two per semester. This mean we took entire courses on Genesis 1–2:4, on Abraham's call in Genesis 12:1-4, and on Jeremiah 31, Exodus 1–2, Psalms 1–2 and others. In each of his courses he included relevant rabbinic exegesis, New Testament use of the Old Testament, and the church fathers' interpretations. Daniel imparted his confidence that God speaks good news now as he accompanied us in our reading, making our hearts burn like those of the disciples of Emmaus, and inspiring us to want to do this with others. In alignment with Vischer and Lys he demonstrated through detailed exegesis of Old Testament texts how God's most total revelation in Jesus both fulfills and explains these Scriptures, making them come alive through the Holy Spirit in our lives and diverse contexts.

While living in France, Gracie and I traveled to Honduras every summer, spending several weeks sharing our learning with Tierra Nueva's Honduran leadership and leading Bible studies in rural villages before returning for classes in the fall. We pursued our studies in France with the vision of bringing the best scholarship to the service of the least in a deliberate effort to bridge the divide between the academy and the poor. Our experience of Daniel's rare blend of scholarship and pastoral sensitivity, which you will see for yourself in his books, contributed to us feeling called back to the church, into ordained ministry, and back to the US to teach and minister there. I benefited from having Daniel as my dissertation supervisor and continued to integrate regular study into our ministry of accompanying immigrants and inmates when we launched Tierra Nueva in Washington State.

Daniel Bourguet's writings are like high-quality wine extracted from vineyards planted in challenged soil. Born in 1946 in Aumessas, a small village in the Cévennes region of France, Daniel grew up in the heartland of Huguenot Protestantism, which issued from the Reformation in the sixteenth century. He pursued studies of theology at the IPT in Montpellier, including study in Germany, Switzerland and at the Ecole Biblique in Jerusalem. In lieu of military service, Daniel served as a teacher in Madagascar for a year. He was ordained as a pastor in the Église Réformée de France in 1972, serving parishes from 1973 to 1987. Daniel wrote his doctoral dissertation[5] while serving as a full-time parish pastor—a common practice in minority Protestant France, where teaching positions are scarce and pastors are in high demand. This practice often proves fruitful for ordinary Christians and theologians alike, deepening reflection and anchoring theologians in the church and world.

During our residential studies in Montpellier from 1988 to 1991, Gracie and I witnessed Daniel's interest in the early monastics and fathers of the Eastern Church grow. In 1991 Daniel became prior of La Fraternité Spirituelle des

5. See Daniel Bourguet, Des métaphores de Jérémie, Paris : J. Gabalda, 1987

Veilleurs (Spiritual Fraternity of the Watchpersons) and felt called to be a full-time monk, leaving the IPT in 1995 for a year in a Cistercian monastery in Lyon before moving to his current site in Les Cévennes in 1996.

Joy, simplicity, and mercy are the three pillars of Les Veilleurs, an association of laypeople and pastors founded by French Reformed pastor Wilfred Monod in 1923 (with a Francophone membership of four hundred in 2013). Members of this fellowship commit to pursuing daily rhythms of prayer and Scripture reading, including noontime recitation of the Beatitudes, Friday meditation on the cross, regular engagement with a faith community on Sundays, and spiritual retreats and reading that benefits from universal devotional and monastic practices. Les Veilleurs has served to nourish renewal in France and influenced the founding of communities such as Taizé. Under Daniel Bourguet's leadership Les Veilleurs thrived. As a member of Les Veilleurs myself I attended many of his annual retreats, witnessing and experiencing the vitality of this movement firsthand.

Since Daniel's departure from his professorship at the IPT in 1995, his teaching and writing have focused primarily on equipping ordinary Christians to grow spiritually through engaging in devotional practices such as prayer, Scripture reading and contemplation. Other works that will hopefully appear in English include reflections on asceticism, silence, daily prayer and the Trinity. All but three of Daniel's twenty-five or so books are based on spiritual retreats he offered to pastors and retreatants with Les Veilleurs. He has offered retreats to Roman Catholic, Orthodox, and Protestant communities throughout France and Francophone Europe and is widely read and appreciated as a theologian who bridges divergent worlds and nourishes faithful Christian practice in France. Daniel Bourguet made his first and only visit to the United States in 2005, offering a spiritual retreat in Washington State. He accompanied me to Honduras on that same trip just after Hurricane Katrina ravaged the country, teaching Tierra Nueva's leaders and accompanying me as I led Bible studies and ministered in rural communities.

Daniel left his role as prior in 2012 and now continues his daily offices, receives many seekers for personal retreats, and offers occasional retreats where he lives and writes. In alignment with the early monastic commitment to manual labor, Daniel weaves black and white wool tapestries of illustrations of biblical stories done by pastor and painter Henri Lindegaard. Daniel's unique contribution includes his Trinitarian approach to biblical interpretation, wherein he reads Scripture informed by the early church fathers with special sensitivity to how texts bear witness directly and indirectly to Jesus, the Father and the Holy Spirit.

Daniel Bourguet models an approach to Scripture and spirituality that is desperately needed in our times. He reads the Bible with great confidence in God's goodness, discovering through careful reading, prayer, and contemplation insights that feed faith and inspire practice. Daniel's deliberate reading in communion with the church fathers brings the wisdom of the ages to nourish the body of Christ today. His tender love for people who come to him for spiritual support as well as the larger church and world informs every page of his writing. May you find in this book refreshment, strength, and inspiration for your journey as you are drawn into deeper encounters with God.

Bob Ekblad
Mount Vernon, WA

PREFACE

THIS BOOK REPRISES STUDIES GIVEN IN SEPTEMBER 2001 AT Pomeyrol during a retreat held for *La Fraternité spirituelle des Veilleurs*. At a retreat, as with preaching, bibliographic references are left aside; they might have had a place as marginal notes, but I prefer to keep them to a minimum, wanting to stay close to the style of a retreat; the reader is invited to take part in a retreat through this book.

The people present at the retreats were believers, Christians, and the reader will see that this is assumed. Nothing has been changed from the retreat, which means that a reader who is not a believer is bound to feel uncertain at times and questions are sure to arise; it needs to be understood that going on a retreat is to retire from the world for a time to be face to face with God, and the teaching at a retreat is a means to that encounter; for this, a person would have to be a believer. You need to know this before starting to read the book; I am speaking here as if at a retreat, to a reader who is a believer.

Finally, again as if on a retreat, I have kept the elements of an oral style. You are addressed here as a "reader friend," as in a dialogue, a dialogue which doesn't propose to be more than an overture to the most sublime of dialogues, dialogue with God.

So there we are, my reader friend! May your dialogue with God find something here to nourish it.

1

THE PRAYER IN JOHN 17

On the eve of his death, that final evening, Jesus spoke at length to his disciples; he spoke freely to them about everything that was on his heart, as we do in a farewell speech to our loved ones. He spoke to them about his Father, about the Holy Spirit, about themselves, the world . . . It all took place in an atmosphere of intimate trust, so the disciples had no hesitation in interrupting him at many points to raise the questions that came to mind.

"After speaking in this way," St John tells us, "Jesus lifted up his eyes to heaven" (17:1). This movement of the eyes was enough for the disciples to understand; Jesus was about to pray (cf. John 11:41; Mark 6:41). Then they were silent; no longer was anyone going to ask questions or presume to interrupt. The silence took on an increased intensity as the disciples became aware of the presence of the person to whom Jesus was about to address his prayer: God was there!

God was, indeed, there, enveloped in silence. He was quiet so as to attentively welcome Jesus' prayer. The disciples were silent, not wishing to disturb the encounter between their master and the Lord. The disciples and God were steeped in this mutual silence, turned towards

Jesus who was about to pray. The disciples attention was extremely keen . . . God seemed so close!

How much time unfolded between the instant Jesus raised his eyes to heaven and the first word of his prayer? I don't know, but the moment seems to be full of eternity . . .

Then Jesus prayed

Jesus' prayer . . . ! What a mystery; an abyss! A mystery so great that the Evangelists did no more than suggest it at a distance, evoking it, but without any attempt to indicate its depth.

The first time Jesus prayed in public was the day of his baptism. On this day, Luke tells us very soberly, "He prayed" (3:21). What else indeed would he be doing in the midst of a crowd called by the Baptist to penitence, that is, to prayer? Certainly, Jesus was praying, like all the penitents in the crowd; nevertheless, his prayer must have been very different since heaven opened as soon as he began! Heaven opened! Nothing similar had ever happened in Israel! Up to this point in the people's history, if at times heaven had opened, it was the opening which led to prayer. Here the set up was reversed; it was the prayer of Jesus which brought the opening of heaven! Surely, no man had ever prayed like this man.

What might Jesus have said in his prayer to cause heaven to open like this? We don't know! The Gospel doesn't tell us what he said, not a word! Jesus' prayer is an unfathomable mystery . . .

That day a voice was heard from heaven, speaking to Jesus: "You are my beloved Son, on whom I have placed all my affection" (Luke 3:22). Jesus' prayer was therefore the prayer of a son to his father, the prayer of the well-beloved Son to his Father. We understand why the content of the prayer is not given to us; it is an intimate concern of God, between the Father and the Son.

On that day the Holy Spirit came down from heaven, from the Father to the Son, not as an outsider to the divine intimacy, but on the contrary, as a party to that intimacy. In fact, as he descends from the Father to the Son, the Spirit is revealed as being close to the Father from whom he proceeds and to whom he listens in silence, and equally close to the Son, to whom he joins himself and whose silence he shares. The intimacy between the Father and the Son includes the Holy Spirit. Jesus' prayer is the prayer of the Son to the Father in the intimacy of the Spirit. This is the unfathomable mystery of Jesus' prayer at the heart of the Trinity.

Hidden prayers

What was Jesus' experience prior to his baptism, that he should reach such a peak of prayer? Before his baptism there were thirty years of hidden life, which no doubt means thirty years of hidden prayer. How many times had heaven opened during those thirty years? We don't know! O, the bottomless mystery of this hidden prayer, buried deep in the Trinity!

Following his baptism, Jesus seems to have wished to continue with some of the customs of his past life; he would go apart, alone, for prayer. Thus we learn that he would withdraw secretly, to one side, to pray in the wilderness (Mark 1:15) or on some mountain (Matt 14:23), at times for entire nights (Luke 6:12). The Gospels surround this prayer with silence, underlining its mystery.

Prayer at the transfiguration

One particular day, Jesus took with him three of his disciples, Peter, James and John, undoubtedly the three closest. He took them "apart to a high mountain" (Matt 17:1). "Apart," as was his custom when he wished to pray. "To a high mountain," as he did at night to devote himself to prayer. Luke is alone in providing this last piece information, so it is not surprising when he tells us that on this day in particular, with his three disciples, Jesus went up into the mountain "to pray" (9:28).

What did Jesus say in his prayer that day? Again, we don't know; Luke doesn't tell us. Perhaps the three disciples knew no more either because Jesus may well have prayed silently. What the disciples did know, however, is that while he prayed he was transfigured (Luke 9:29). "His face shone like the sun," Matthew tells us, "and his garments became as white as pure light" (17:2). Is this how it was each time that Jesus went off by himself alone to pray? We know nothing of this — but, why not? At any rate, on this day a voice made itself heard, as at the baptism, but on this occasion, to be heard by the disciples: "This is my beloved Son; hear him" (Mark 9:7).

While he was still praying to his Father, a luminous cloud covered them all in its shadow (Matt 17:5). The verb chosen here "cover with its shadow," discreetly reveals that the luminous cloud was a manifestation of the Holy Spirit. Throughout the rest of the Gospels, the only subject of this verb is the Holy Spirit (see Luke 1:35). It was out of the cloud that the voice of the Father came; again, it is within the cloud that we find the Son engulfed. We see, then, the Father and the Son united in the cloud, united by the Holy

Spirit. Where the contents of Jesus' prayer are not given us, this is because they belong to the intimacy of the Trinity, as on the day of the baptism. O, the unfathomable mystery of the prayer of he who was transfigured, in the depths of trinitarian communion . . .

The prayer of the final evening

On this, the last evening of his life, during the course of his lengthy farewell discourse, Jesus gave his disciples the title of friends (John 15:14–15). It was the first time he had called them this, as if wishing to prepare them to enter into an intimacy as yet unknown to them. At the close of this discourse, when he raises his eyes to heaven, is Jesus about to pray aloud as one might do among friends? This in fact is what he does. The silence of the disciples becomes clear now; it is that of new friends, ready to welcome an intimacy which is about to be unveiled.

It's on the eve of his death, then, that Jesus raises his eyes to heaven in the presence of his friends and drops into their silence the first word of his prayer, "Father . . ."

No one could say whether heaven, hearing this word, was open, but the disciples would have understood that the heart of the Father surely was; they would have understood it in the density of the sovereign silence.

There is no mention in what follows of whether Jesus' face was transfigured, but the disciples would have definitely known that they were immersed in the indescribable light of the Holy Spirit. They would have known it because of the ineffaceable way Jesus' prayer was engraved upon their hearts.

In the Holy Spirit, the disciples listen to the well-beloved Son pray to his Father . . .

1. Father, the hour is come! Glorify your Son, that your Son may glorify you, 2. even as you have given him power over all flesh, that he may give eternal life to those you have given him. 3. This is eternal life, that they may know you, the only true God, and the one you have sent, Jesus Christ. 4. I have glorified you on earth; I have accomplished the work that you gave me to do. 5. And now, Father, glorify me with your own self with the glory I had beside you before the world was made.

6. I have manifested your name to the men you have given me out of the world. They were yours and you gave them to me, and they have kept your word. 7. Now they have known that all you have given me comes from you. 8. I have given them the words you gave me; they have received them; they have truly known that I came from you and they have believed that you sent me.

9. It is for them that I pray. I am not praying for the world, but for those you have given me, because they are yours. 10. All that is mine is yours, and all that is yours is mine. I am glorified in them. 11. I am no longer in the world, but they are in the world. I am coming to you.

Holy Father, keep in your name those you have given me, that they may be one in us. 12. While I was with them in the world, I have kept them in your name. I have kept those you have given me, and not one of them is lost except for the son of perdition, that the Scriptures might be fulfilled.

13. And now I am coming to you, and I say these things in the world that they might have in them my perfect joy. 14. I have given them your word, and the world has hated them since they are not of the world, as I am not of the world. 15. I do not ask that you take them out of the world, but that you preserve them from the Evil One. 16. They are not of the world, as I am not of the world. 17. Sanctify them by your word; your word is truth. 18 As you have sent me into the world, I am sending them into the world. 19. I sanctify myself for them, that they too may be sanctified by the truth.

20. It is not for these alone that I pray, but also for those who will believe in me through their word, 21. that they may be one, as you, Father, you are in me and I am in you, that may also be in us, that the world may believe that you have sent me. 22. I have given them the glory which you have given me, that they may be one as we are one, I in them and you in me, 23. that they may come to perfect unity, and that the world may know that you have sent me and that you have loved them as you have loved me.

24. Father, I will that where I am, those you have given me may be also, that they may see my glory, the glory that you gave me before the foundation of the world. 25. Righteous Father, the world has not known you; but I have known you, and they have learned that you have sent me. 26. I have made your name known to them and I will make it known, that the love with which you have loved me may be in them, and that I may be in them.

Jesus prays in the presence of his disciples

"Father," Jesus says as he begins his prayer. No one in Israel had ever felt able to address God in this way, but for the disciples it was no surprise because Jesus had never stopped speaking of God in such terms. Little by little they had been discovering the depth of love this word might mean on Jesus' lips, even if in the heart of the people it provoked violent reactions. Jesus, indeed, was to have been stoned because of it (see John 10: 30–31).

"Father," says Jesus. While the disciples had already heard Jesus pray like this, it was such a rarity (11:41) and the prayers so short, that they had no more than glimpsed the intimacy of which Jesus had nonetheless spoken from time to time; he had told them for example, "I am in the Father and the Father is in me" (14:10), or again, "I and the Father are one" (10:30). It was one thing to hear the Son talk about his intimacy with the Father, and quite another, something overwhelming, to actually be a witness to that intimacy. It was this complete overturning that the disciples now knew as they heard him say, "Father, you are in me and I am in you" (17:21).

To this was added further astonishment; until this point the disciples had never heard Jesus pray to the Father on their behalf. They knew nothing of the way in which Jesus spoke of them to his Father in the intimacy of his prayer. What they were now discovering, on this eve of their master's death, had much to utterly change them. Jesus speaks of them in terms saturated with an immense love: "You have loved them as you have loved me" (17:23). Then he asks his Father not to stop loving them in this way: "May the love with which you have loved me be in them and I in them too" (17:26).

"The love with which you have loved me"; that is, the love which split the heavens on the day of my baptism and which transfigured me on the mountain, may this love, Father, burn in them as it burns in me . . .

Jesus ponders[1] the impact of his words on his disciples. His prayer is suddenly arrested on these words without any form of conclusion, no Amen . . . nothing but silence . . . It's a silence the depth of which is commensurate with the love of which he has been speaking. Jesus has just committed the disciples into the heart of the Father; then he is silent. It is the silence of intimacy between Father and Son. The disciples understand by this silence the extent of the love with which they are loved and discover that their place is in intimacy with God . . . The disciples then become quite silent, allowing themselves to be wrapped around by the silence of the Father, the better to enjoy this intimacy with God in the profundity of the Son's prayer.

The Holy Spirit is silent too. Not once was he mentioned in the prayer, but he is there, as he is always present in the intimacy of the Father and Son. The Spirit is there in the hearts of the disciples and is silent there within them, leading them into silent adoration . . .

"Father," the Son had said in the silence of the Spirit! The silence of the Spirit is a silence of love; the listening ear of the Father is a listening ear of love; the prayer of the Son is a prayer of love: a Trinity of love enflaming the hearts of the disciples with love, hearts that now burn in the silence of adoration . . .

Reader friend, with what mysteries have we to do here! May the Holy Spirit envelop us in his silence as in a luminous cloud, enabling us to enter, if only a little, into the mystery of Jesus' prayer, into the mystery of his intimacy with the Father, into the mystery of Trinitarian love . . . In quietness, we worship . . .

1. Fr. *se doute bien* ie questions or doubts.

He prays with his friends

When Jesus begins to pray aloud in front of his disciples on this final evening of his life, it is not a moment for unrestrained emotional outpouring nor for erudite teaching on how to pray. Jesus is talking to his closest friends and now draws them in wonderful simplicity into his prayer. He doesn't see them either as outsiders to his spiritual life, or as merely witnesses to the intimacy of his prayer, but as those with whom he wishes to pray, those who can enter into his prayer to such an extent that the intimacy of his prayer also becomes theirs, and they too become beings of prayer. Jesus accompanies his disciples, leading them into the Father's heart along the pathway of prayer.

The whole opening of John 17 demonstrates the great care with which Jesus involves the disciples in his praying. In fact the prayer is very much Jesus' own, one which he expresses unequivocally in the first person. Notwithstanding, strangely, the opening of the prayer, up to verse 3, is so stated that it would be better understood on the lips of the disciples than Jesus. Indeed, these first three verses speak of Jesus in the third person, as though it were really a prayer of the disciples: "Father, the hour is come! Glorify your Son, that your Son may glorify you, according as you have given him power over all flesh, that he may give eternal life to all those you have given him. This is eternal life, that they may know you, the only true God, and the one you have sent, Jesus Christ."

Nowhere else in the Gospels does Jesus speak of himself as "Jesus Christ"! This expression is a formula for the confession of faith by the disciples and not a way for Jesus to speak. It is often the case that Jesus speaks of himself as "the Son of Man" (Matt 16:27; Mark 8:31; Luke 9:44; John 3:14 . . .) or, again, he styles himself "the Son of God"

(John 3:16). To find the words "Jesus Christ" on Jesus' lips is so exceptional that some modern commentators have thought that this opening to John 17 is a gloss. This judgment seems to me too fast! I believe rather that, for Jesus, the best way to involve the disciples in his prayer was to pray on their terms.

Jesus, then, begins his prayer by giving the disciples the words that should really be their prayer on this, the threshold of his passion: "Father, the hour is come, glorify your Son . . ." Then he continues his prayer in a more personal way, in the first person, but always aloud for his disciples to hear, so that they could pray with him, for the moment at least.

As he skillfully places his prayer onto the lips of his disciples, Jesus does the same for us, so that we in turn might be involved. In this way, Jesus manages to be both perfectly present in his prayer and somewhat retired, effaced, to birth us into his prayer and thus lead us into the heart of God.

Intimacy with the Father

Having involved us in the intimacy of his prayer, Jesus also involves us in his intimacy with the Father. As he in fact places this prayer on our lips, he also places there the very first word of the prayer, a simple vocative, but a vocative so extraordinary that it represents in itself alone a real revolution in the history of prayer: "Father."

"Father," says Jesus, with the simplicity of someone who has never prayed any other way.

"Father," he says, without using any possessive pronoun. Not "my Father," which would leave us outside his prayer, not "our Father," which might include us by force, but simply "Father," as a humble and discreet invitation, allowing each person the joy of discovering that this word might become on their lips "my Father" or "our Father," and discovering too how close the word brings us to the one of whom it speaks.

"Father": by having us pray like this, Christ brings us to the discovery of our identity as sons, daughters, as children of God! Wonderful discovery! What an amazing gift Christ gives us as he involves us in his prayer. To be a child to God: this is the deep mystery of our being, our true identity.

"Father"; we hear the word both on the lips of Jesus and on our own, thus discovering the extraordinary but discreet closeness between Jesus and ourselves; his Father and our Father, quite simply! (cf John 20.17) This simplicity immerses us in wonderment.

"Father": Jesus is not reducing the disciples to the level of children by having them pray in this way any more than he presents himself to them as somehow infantile! There is no one more adult than Christ on this the eve of his death. An adult says "father" to his father right up to his last day. Jesus advances his disciples along the road of adult life right into the heart of the Father.

"Father": the vocative reverberates from one end to the other of this prayer (5, 11, 21, 24, 25), also modulating into "holy Father" (v 11) and "righteous Father" (v 25). From the first word through to the end of the prayer, Jesus includes us little by little further into a wonderful and profound intimacy with the Father. This intimacy with the Father is not a good that is jealously guarded by Jesus, but a treasure of love that he offers to share.

From the first word, and with that word alone, Jesus involves us at once in the mystery of prayer and the mystery of God's fatherhood. He causes us to contemplate the Father, his Father, our Father . . . When we reach the final words of the prayer without any closing formula, with no Amen , with no continuation other than silence, Jesus leaves us in silent contemplation of the Father . . .

If we don't know how to pray, this is no doubt because we have not yet sufficiently entered into the mystery of the Father. Before we pronounce the first word of our prayer, it is good to take time to consider that we are addressing our Father and to take stock of the depth of intimacy into which we are thereby plunged. Before pronouncing the first word of prayer, we should take the time to think about the Father, that is, to look lovingly towards him. We can then enter into prayer with love, with the humble and discreet love which discovers intimacy with someone. It is into our contemplative silence that Jesus with delicacy deposits his filial prayer, for it to there become ours.

The influence of the Holy Spirit

"Father": to pray like this means learning from Christ and recognizing oneself as a child of God. Now, welcoming this as an effective reality in our life is only possible with the help of the Holy Spirit, who comes into our hearts to attest that we truly are children of God (Rom 8:16). As the apostle Paul says so justly, only the Holy Spirit can enable us to say "Father" in our prayer; he alone enables us to say it with such depth of intimacy, even helping us to call him "Abba," as did Jesus (Mark 14:36), which is to say "Father"; or even better, "papa" (Rom 8:15, Gal 4:6) — "abba" is the affectionate diminutive of "ab," which means "father."

If we don't know how to pray, it must be because we have not yet entered sufficiently into the mystery of

13

the Holy Spirit. Before beginning to speak in prayer, it is good to observe a silence, the silence which opens us to the silence of the Holy Spirit, so that we allow the name of the Father, "Abba," to rise up within us, as whispered by the Spirit. Into our silence the Spirit enters silently to lead us into prayer, and reveal to us that we are children of God. In this way our heart begins to burn as the Spirit moves quietly into our silence, enabling us to pray.

In the mystery of the Trinity

With this word "Father" spoken in the Holy Spirit and with the Son, Jesus in the end is bringing us into the unfathomable mystery of the Trinity. In just one word, the very first of his prayer, Jesus immerses us in an infinite mystery. Right on the threshold of his prayer Jesus conducts us all at once into the mystery of prayer, into the mystery of who we are, and into the mystery of the Trinity! The Trinity is not simply the final goal of our spiritual progress, but is already available to us for this, the first step in our life of prayer . . .

If we don't know how to pray, this is no doubt because we have not yet sufficiently entered into the mystery of the Trinity. Before beginning to speak in prayer, it is good for us to ponder the Father in the mystery of the Trinity. We will never have a sufficient depth of silence to get to the bottom of this opening word!

The Triune God leads us into prayer, and in prayer we enter the mystery of this Trinity . . .

When we come to the final word of this prayer that lacks a formal conclusion, has no Amen, and has no continuation other than silence, we are immersed in the silence of the Son, a silence which is united with the silence of the Father and the silence of the Spirit. It is a silence that unites the three persons of the Trinity, the silence of deep communion, the silence of intimacy between the Father, the Son and the Holy Spirit, an unfathomable intimacy! Intimacy consists more of silence than of words. The greater it is, the quieter it becomes, and the silence gives each word extraordinary depth. As he inducts us into the silence of the Trinity, Jesus graces us with entrance into the communion of Trinitarian love, into Trinitarian intimacy.

From the first word until the silence into which it impels us, Jesus' prayer is a burning bush which enflames our heart when we enter into it with him. Reader friend, may this silence of intimacy also become for us the silence of contemplation and adoration . . .

The final prayer

In relation to John's Gospel as a whole, the prayer of chapter 17 is Jesus' final prayer. Indeed, in the passage which immediately follows and in events in the garden of Gethsemane (ch. 18), no allusion is made to Jesus' praying, whereas his prayers are mentioned in detail in the other three Gospels. In what follows in John's account of the Passion, after Gethsemane, nothing further is said of Jesus praying, not even on the cross; this is quite amazing when we consider the place Jesus' praying occupies in the other three Gospels (see Matt 27:46; Mark 15:34; Luke 23:34, 46). When, in John, Jesus says on the cross, for example, "I thirst" (19:28) or "all is accomplished" (19:30), there is nothing that would allow us to affirm that the words are spoken to his Father. It does seem then that John 17, according to this evangelist, was really Jesus' last prayer. It is certainly the case that it is the final time we hear Jesus say, "Father."

As a final prayer, it is most astonishing, and has a very particular profile and depth. In one way, in fact, the prayer of John 17 fits in perfectly with all Jesus is going through on this, the eve of his death. It is remarkably well integrated into the farewell discourse (chs. 13–16), which it concludes, and the account of the Passion (chs. 18–19), which it introduces. "Father, the hour is come," says Jesus, knowing full well that the hour in question is that of the cross. "I am coming to you," he says twice (17:11, 13), thinking of the cross as a passageway leading back to the Father. This all locates Jesus firmly on this earth, shortly before his death. It is exactly because he is on the earth that Jesus "lifted up his eyes to heaven" to pray.

Nevertheless, we also find alongside this, in the same prayer, expressions which again surprise us because they seem to situate Jesus as having already been to the cross and no longer on this earth! "When I was with them," he says, speaking of his disciples, even while he is still praying with them! "I am no longer in the world," he says again (17:11), when he surely still is and has yet to be crucified! "Father, my desire is that, where I am, those you have given me may also be, that they may see my glory" (17.24). What does this "where I am" mean? If Jesus is in a place where his disciples can contemplate his glory, it must be that he is already in glory, which is to say at the right hand of the Father, in the bosom of the Father (1:18), right where he was from all eternity, before the world was made (17:5), and for all eternity to come.

By expressing himself as he does, situating himself both before and after the cross, Jesus gives this prayer a particular character which links it both with time and eternity, both fully fitting into the history of the Passion as well as already belonging entirely to eternity.

16

An eternal prayer

"I will that where I am they also may be with me"; by speaking like this, Jesus locates himself where he alone can be said to be, in the eternal relationship with the Father which meant he could say before the cross what he could say of all eternity: "I am in the Father and the Father is in me" (14:10). The present tense of the verb "to be" is the present of eternity. "There, where I am," belongs to the same present; it is the present of "I am who I am," pronounced by God to Moses as a statement of his deep identity (Exod 3:14).

"I am no longer in the world . . . There where I am, I will that they too may be with me"; through these expressions, Jesus' prayer is located fully in eternity, which further means that he is always praying this way. Today still, Jesus is living the now of eternity and is praying this prayer for our benefit. Reader friend, isn't this wonderful? At this very moment he is interceding for us at the right hand of God; he is saying: "Father, I will that, where I am, those you have given me may also be, and that they may behold my glory . . ."; but also, "Father, keep them . . . sanctify them . . . that they may be one as we are one." Just as he prayed on this last evening before the cross while among his disciples, so too he bears us up today in his prayer and will continue to bear us until the day of its complete fulfilment . . .

No doubt it is because of the prayer's eternal nature that it has no formal conclusion, no Amen; Jesus prays this way eternally, or, at least, as long as the world exists.

Understanding John 17 in this way gives wonderful substance to what Paul writes in Romans: "Christ intercedes for us at the right hand of the Father" (8:34). Christ's intercession is a present reality. "Because he abides eternally . . . he ever lives to make intercession" (Heb 7:24–25). While the apostle doesn't tell us the terms in which Christ intercedes for us before the Father, John's Gospel does; he is praying for us just as he prayed for his disciples on the eve of his death; that's why this is his "final" prayer, his ultimate prayer, the prayer that has no end.

When we pray, we are not taking up the baton from a Christ who ceased to pray two thousand years ago; no, we join in with his prayer, which remains a present reality. We pray with him. As we pray John 17, we are birthed in prayer, into the eternity of the Son's prayer.

When Christ affords us entrance into communion with him in his prayer, when he prays with us through to the final verse and then immerses us in his silence, in this silence we are also given a taste of eternity; we behold the Son at the right hand of the Father, ourselves indwelt by the Spirit who opens us to this contemplation.

Now we can murmur softly an "amen" which has a certain savor of eternity . . .

The priestly prayer

The prayer of John 17 is commonly termed the "high priestly prayer," and this seems thoroughly judicious to me. I believe, in fact, that it can be related to what is said in Heb 7:24–26, where there is a discussion of Jesus' intercession in his role as priest, indeed as high priest. This high priest, the epistle tells us, is "holy," which complements what Jesus himself said to his Father: "I sanctify myself for them" (John 17:19). This prayer of Jesus is eternal, as we have noted, and this too fits with the epistle, with its description of Jesus as the eternal high priest: "He remains for eternity . . . He ever lives to intercede" (Heb 7:21, 24). The prayer of John 17 is therefore exactly the prayer Jesus speaks in his capacity as high priest. It follows that when I speak of the "priestly prayer," reader friend, please understand I am referring to John 17.

The outline of the priestly prayer is easy to see: firstly, Jesus speaks of himself (1–5), then he prays at length for his disciples (6–19); he continues his intercession by including those who would be converted thanks to the disciples' preaching (20–23); and finishes by speaking again of his disciples (24–26).

In the central section devoted to the disciples, Jesus essentially asks two things of his Father: "keep them" (17:11), and "sanctify them" (17:17). I am struck by the way, in asking this, Jesus proposes that his Father intervene in logical continuation of what he himself was doing. "I have kept them," he says in summary of his entire earthly ministry (17:12); "keep them," he asks of his Father, picking up the same verb (17:11 and 15), so that his work, interrupted by the cross, might be perpetuated eternally thanks to the intervention of his Father. Just as he had kept his disciples by love, so he looks to his Father for the same love to continue to keep them (17:26), that they might at all be times preserved from the Evil One (17:15). Jesus does not abandon those who have been entrusted to him; he prays eternally for them, entrusting them to the one who, better than any, is able to keep them eternally.

The same harmonious complementarity is evident in Jesus' other request to his Father. "Sanctify them," Jesus prays (17:17); then he adds, "I have sanctified myself that they may be sanctified" (17:19). In sanctifying himself, Jesus clearly has in view the sanctification of his disciples; when death necessarily interrupts his work, he then entrusts it to his Father, for him to continue.

So, I am struck that Jesus looks to his Father to intervene and work in the same way he had done, so that the Father's work and his are the continuation of each other, in harmony. The prayer is not a standing down on his part but the offering up of his life's work. We need to realize that things are often very different with us: our prayers are often a sort of abdication; we ask God to intervene where we have laid down our arms, given up. Jesus teaches us here that prayer is in no way an abdication of responsibility; rather it is a calling upon God to work in the same direction as we have been going; it's a way of entrusting our activities to God, linking them up with him because without him we can do nothing.

Sanctify them

Each of the two requests Jesus addresses to his Father are there for us to meditate, and they could each form the subject of lengthy discussion. I am going to stay just with the second of them, and it will open up for us extraordinary horizons. Although it is only the second of the two on Jesus lips, it is not for that of less importance; perhaps quite the opposite!

At the outset of the priestly prayer, as he prays for himself, Jesus addresses himself to the Father, saying quite simply to him, "Father" (17:1, 5). Then, when he prays for his disciples, he slightly modifies the vocative, changing from "Father" to "Holy Father" (17:11). This is the first time Jesus speaks to the Father like this; he does it nowhere else. He does so here for a precise reason; it is, it seems to me, to introduce and prepare the request that he holds closest to his heart: "Holy Father, sanctify them." When Jesus sanctifies himself that the disciples may be sanctified too, it is not his own holiness that he sets to the fore but the holiness of his Father; we see here the humility of Jesus in his not saying "sanctify them because I sanctify myself on their behalf," but simply, "Father, you who are holy, make them partakers of your holiness." Reader friend, it is in the school of humility that prayer is learned.

God alone is holy

The uses of the adjective "holy" in John's Gospel are thoroughly remarkable and merit our attention. The adjective, in fact, is strictly reserved for God. It is applied to the Father only in the verse we are looking at. We also find it just once to refer to the Son, in a vital text where Peter makes a confession of faith which involves the whole Church: "We believe and we know that you are the holy one of God" (6:69). Finally, all the other uses qualify the Holy Spirit, who alone is termed "Holy Spirit" (1:33, 7:39, 14:26 and 20:22).

In short, in this Gospel, the Father is holy, the Son is holy, the Spirit is holy; this is the truth, that God alone is holy.

This way of using the word "holy" contrasts strongly with what we find in the first three Gospels, where the following are also termed "holy": Jerusalem, the holy city (Matt 4:5, 27:53); the Temple, the holy place (Matt 24:15); the angels (Mark 8:38, Luke 9:26); certain men (Matt 27:52), of whom John the Baptist is one in particular (Mark 6:20); and again, God's covenant (Luke 1:72). Meanwhile, in John too there is mention of Jerusalem (2:13 . . .), the Temple (2:14 . . .), the angels (1:51, 20:12), John the Baptist (1:19, 35 . . .) . . . but never is there any mention of them being holy.

It is therefore very clearly the case that in John's Gospel God alone is holy, only the Trinity is holy. When Peter confesses that Jesus is "the holy one of God," we note that he uses the definite article to specify that he is the one and only holy one of God. In addition to the Son, indeed, there is no one holy apart from the Father and the Spirit.

Given that holiness is only to be found in God, it is therefore of God alone that it can be sought on behalf of the disciples. At the same time, though, we must consider the extraordinary nature of the request; Jesus asks for his disciples what belongs to God alone, the very thing that unites him with the Father and the Spirit. He wishes to introduce us into what he shares with his Father and the Spirit. What an extraordinary request this is, honoring us to the highest degree: "Holy Father, make them partakers of our holiness."

Sanctification

If God alone is holy, it can be no surprise to see, as we do in John's Gospel, that God alone sanctifies. The rare uses of the verb "to sanctify" in the Gospel do indeed run in this direction, in accordance with the biblical logic which says that only the already holy can sanctify.

When Jesus says that he "sanctifies himself" that the disciples might be sanctified (17:19), it is the "holy one of God" who is speaking. In saying that he sanctifies himself when he is already holy, Jesus is saying, it seems to me, that he is fully aware of his own holiness and that he assumes[2] this in order to prepare himself to share this holiness with his disciples.

The only other use of the verb "sanctify" in this Gospel is in 10:36, where we find that the Father has sanctified the

---

2. "Assume" in the sense of adopting a role, putting on a mantle. (Trans.)

Son; this clearly throws into relief the fact that the source of holiness is in the Father. Here we see why it is to the Father that the Son turns to seek the sanctification of the disciples: *as you have sanctified me, sanctify them too . . .*

Only a holy person can sanctify! This biblical truth rests on the idea that holiness is transmitted and propagated by contact. To be in contact with someone holy renders you holy. To ask the Father to sanctify the disciples means asking that he be in contact with them, which is to say, in close relationship, in love fellowship with them, in that relationship which Jesus describes in the astonishing formulation, "you in me and I in you" (17:21). It is from this intimate communion of love that sanctification of the Son by the Father flows. Asking the Father to sanctify the disciples amounts to saying this to him: "Holy Father, may they be in you and you in them."

Be holy

In the Old Testament the following invitation of God's is recorded: "Be holy, for I am holy" (Lev 19:2, restated in 1 Pet 1:16). This does not mean "become holy by your own efforts by which you might approach me, the holy one," but, "become holy by approaching me, the holy one."

"Be holy," the Father requires. "Sanctify them," adds the Son. It's then that the Holy Spirit draws near to us in silence to lead us along the way of holiness.

What exactly does "sanctify" mean?

The verb can mean "consecrate," in the sense of "set apart." This is what we find in, for example, Exodus 13:2: "The Lord said to Moses, 'Consecrate to me every first born.'"

If this was all it meant, to set apart, John would have used the verb with other subjects than God. However, by making God the only subject, John accords the verb a stronger meaning than "set apart" or "consecrate." For him, "to sanctify" means "to transmit holiness," "to cause participation in holiness," in accordance with the second sense the word can have. Thus, in Matt 23:17, for example, the temple "sanctifies" the gold that is brought there, because the Temple, itself holy, transmits holiness to the gold by contact. The same is true for the altar which "sanctifies" through its holiness the offering which is placed on it (Matt 23:19).

We see that with the Temple and the altar, holiness is transmitted by contact. In sanctifying some person, the Father, then, does more than just set apart; he enters into contact in order to impart his holiness.

"Holy, holy, holy is the Lord," the seraphim in the Temple proclaim (Isa 6:3). When the proclamation of this holiness causes the doors of the Temple to shake (6:4), this is because holiness is a formidable life force, a power so great that it chases away evil and leaves it no place; it excludes evil to the point of causing it to disappear and the sinner with it. This is why it is such a tremendous thing for a sinner to approach the Holy One; this can bring death if the Lord is not gracious to him. When he sanctifies someone, God communicates his life and purifies from all sin; viewed in this way, holiness includes moral perfection.

Where the holiness of the Temple or the altar is transmitted by physical contact, God's holiness at a moral level is not transmitted by physical contact but by the spiritual communion of love. When he sanctifies us, God imparts his holiness and moral perfection as we are brought into the intimacy of his own love fellowship. However, since this love fellowship allows room for man's liberty, God accompanies sanctification with an invitation which respects this liberty: "Be holy, as I am holy."

"Sanctify them," the Son asks of the Father. It is with a view to satisfying his Son that the Father responds with an invitation addressed to the disciples in their liberty: "Be holy, for I am holy." Paul echoes this invitation when he says to the Romans, "You are called to be holy (saints)" (1:7).

The dynamics of holiness

"You are called to be holy," Paul writes. Elsewhere he says, "You are holy" (Col 3:12)! If we are already holy but are also called to become holy, holiness must be a process, a road with its source in God and its accomplishment in him too. This is just how things are. A communion of love is a life process, taking place in time and evolving in time. Holiness is a progressive pathway, from a nascent holiness on through to total holiness. For this reason the apostle says, "May the God of peace sanctify you wholly" (1 Thess 5:23). Here Paul has in view fullness of holiness, knowing full well that the road that leads there is paved with hindrances, with advances and retreats . . .

Along this way of holiness, each step is taken in synergy with the holy Trinity. The Spirit sanctifies (Rom 15:16); which is to say that our holiness grows with the increasing activity of the Spirit in us. He it is, we can say, who transforms us from holiness to holiness. The Son too sanctifies (1 Cor 1:2), and our holiness grows with his increasing activity in us. Finally, the Father sanctifies, just as Jesus asked him on our behalf.

Where we have to speak of synergy, it is because God sanctifies us but all the while with the invitation that we participate in the sanctification: "Be holy." God gives, even as he instructs. We are called to participate, knowing all the while that our efforts are impelled, sustained and seen to their end by the Father, the Son and the Spirit, who together never cease to sanctify us. Let us only, reader friend, not put any obstacle in the way of God's working within us, handing ourselves entirely over to him!

The synergy of this process of sanctification is wonderfully expressed by a verse from Revelation, which, if it is to be translated properly, needs a word of explanation: "Let him that is holy continue to sanctify himself" (Rev 22.11),[3] following the translation of the TOB, which emphasizes the effective participation of man. However, the Greek verb is here employed in a form which also has a passive sense, so the verse could also be translated as "let him that is holy continue to be sanctified," that is, "sanctified by God," emphasizing now the effective participation of God. It's the combination of the two translations that needs to be borne in mind, and this is not something that can be achieved by translation alone: let the saint be busy about his own sanctification, trusting all along that God alone sanctifies!

Holiness is found in God, who is its source and its accomplishment, but man's part is included, slight though it might be and insignificant in comparison with God's, the God who longs for it, calls for it and respects it. "Be holy because I am making you holy" is what we might understand in God's invitation to us.

3. "Let him that is holy be holy still" KJV. DB's discussion concerns the French translation he uses here. TOB is the *Traduction oecuménique de la Bible*. (Trans.)

Sanctified for the world's sake

Why, though, sanctify the disciples? With what end in view?

Before answering this question, which stems from our reading of John 17, we need to turn back to John 10:36, which speaks of Christ's sanctification by God and gives the reason for it. Here the answer is clear: God sanctifies the Son in order to send him into the world. Christ, in fact, is "the one who the Father has sanctified and sent into the world." Well, in John 17, the answer is just as clear: it is also for the purpose of being sent into the world that disciples need to be sanctified. The same expression ("to send into the world") is found in almost the same form in 10:36 and 17:18, except that in 17:18 it is Jesus who does the sending of the disciples into the world: "As you have sent me into the world, so I send them into the world." This is the first time that John's Gospel speaks of the disciples being sent out by Jesus into the world. It is with this mission in mind that the Son turns to the Father: as you have sanctified me to send me into the world, now sanctify those whom I am sending into the world.

The whole thing is quite clear; sanctification is the necessary preliminary to being sent into the world. However this needs to be examined more closely since there is, it seems to me, a paradox of sorts. In one way, in fact, the sanctification of the disciples sets them apart from the world, the world which in itself is entirely profane. Nevertheless, it is exactly in order to send them into this world that Jesus asks for the sanctification of the disciples! What is the nature of the world in Jesus' eyes that would make necessary the sanctification of those who are sent into it?

There are two ways to answer this question since the word "world" has two connotations in John's Gospel. The

27

two responses seem to be contradictory, but we will have to guard ourselves against feeling we have to make a choice between them; they are inseparable from each another and complementary. We need, I believe, to understand, accept, take in and experience the two responses, just as we need to take in and experience the double meaning of "world."

For reasons of clarity, reader friend, I am going to fully set out the first response to this question of sanctification and then keep the second for a further chapter. However, the better to understand the tension between the two, I will briefly indicate both responses here before examining them in depth.

Sanctification by God is tied to his drawing near; it increases as he draws closer, as we have seen. The place *par excellence* of God's presence is the sanctuary, a place sanctified by the presence of the holy God. This means that man must be sanctified if he is to first enter the sanctuary, and then to go further into it. If a disciple needs to be sanctified to go into the world, this is because the world is considered a sanctuary which has been made holy by the God who is in it. This is the first meaning to Jesus' request of his Father: "Sanctify them so that I can send them into the holy place that this world is."

At the same time, though, following a line of thought also to be found in the Bible, man needs to be sanctified if he is to take part in the holy war waged by the holy God in the world. In the Old Testament, a war is seen as holy to the degree that it is conducted by God; everything God does is made holy by his holiness, including war. Therefore, every soldier who takes part in the holy war needs to be sanctified before throwing himself into combat. So, the world is to be considered as a battlefield in which God, together with his people, fights against his adversaries. This is the second meaning to Jesus' request of his Father: "Sanctify them so that I can send them into holy warfare in the world."

The world as a sanctuary! And the world as a battlefield! This, reader friend, is the paradox of the world before which we find ourselves. It is into this paradoxical world that Christ sends us, asking all the while that his Father sanctify us.

2

THE WORLD AS SANCTUARY

IN THIS, THE ONLY PRIESTLY PRAYER, THE WORD "WORLD" is found 18 times, a very considerable number when we realize that in the three other Gospels it is used a total of 15 times! In his high priestly prayer, for Jesus the world is a constant present, and not in a purely negative way.

In itself the Greek word for world, "cosmos," is extremely positive. The word stems from a root which means "to set in order" and so invokes beauty and harmony. The same word also indicates a woman's make-up and finery, and we derive our word cosmetic from it. The world is a place which is ordered, harmonious and so genuinely beautiful.

The beautifying nature of make-up serves a second beauty which far surpasses it; it serves to underline the beauty of a woman. It is not the make-up which makes a woman beautiful; it emphasizes the beauty which is already there. In the same way, the beauty of the cosmos does not have its end in itself; it underlines a beauty which transcends it, in fact a double beauty, the beauty of God and of his image on earth, the human person. God's beauty and man's beauty mutually join together to form a whole, to which attention is called by the beauty of the world.

The foundation of the world

Among the continual references to the world in the high priestly prayer, there is one in which Jesus uses a curious expression, "the foundation of the world" (17:24). This expression has this oddity about it, that it is never used in the Septuagint and must therefore have originated with Jesus himself. The expression was picked up by the authors of the New Testament to the extent that almost all of them echo it, Matthew (25:34), Luke (11:50), Paul (Eph 1:4) and Peter (1 Pet 1:20), as well as references in the letter to the Hebrews (4:3, 9:26) and Revelation (13:8, 17:8). If this large New Testament inventory is not taking up an expression from the Old Testament Greek, it must surely have come from Jesus; so what then does he mean when he speaks of the "foundation of the world"?

I understand that as he speaks of the world's foundation Jesus is talking about creation, but in a way in which the world, the "cosmos" is regarded as a building.

While the expression "the foundation of the world" is something of a novelty on Jesus' lips, the idea of the world being comparable to a building is not new; indeed it is found already present on the Bible's first page.

God founded the sanctuary of the cosmos

Looked at closely, Genesis 1 describes the cosmos as a building, and more precisely as a sanctuary. According to Gen 1, God did not create the world and then later build a temple, but rather created the entire cosmos as a temple, as a space in which everything is holy, without even the smallest tract of profane ground.

In this chapter, the sun and the moon are at no point termed "sun" and "moon," nor are they described as heavenly bodies. They are given the title "lights"[4] (1:14, 15, 16). Now, throughout the rest of the Pentateuch, this word is reserved for the furnishings of the sanctuary; so, if the sun and the moon are lights it is because they belong to the furnishings of a sanctuary on a cosmic scale; the entire cosmos is seen as a sanctuary.

In Gen 1:10, all the waters of the seas together are termed *"miqwé,"* and this can be translated as "reservoir," a term which is particularly used in Judaism for the basin of purification located at the entrance to the sanctuary. So, if the seas together form a vast purifying basin, this is another way of saying that the cosmos is a sanctuary in which this basin is required for access to the dry land where the people are.

In this great cosmic temple, man and woman are then placed as the "image" of God (1:26, 27), which itself is interesting because the word "image" in a holy place is used to designate a statue of God which is to be venerated there (cf Num 33.52, 2 Kgs 11.18 . . .). By speaking of men and women in this way, the Bible makes of them the sole image of God on the earth. God has no need of any statue because man and woman are his image, his sole representation, a perfect visible attestation of his invisible presence. What an immense honor God does humanity. Where God finished his work with the creation of man, it is because it was necessary for the cosmic temple to be finished before he put his image in it; and this image he was eager to "bless" (1:28), thus underlining our unrivalled place among created beings.

4. Or lamps (Trans.)

Then God provides speech for worship[5]

In this cosmic sanctuary created by God, he alone spoke for six days; speech was reserved for him. No one else said anything; words were his, and in the presence of God the whole creation was silent. Furthermore, what he said was not addressed to the creation; when he spoke on the first day, "Let there be light," he was speaking about light, not to it.

The same is true of the following days, until the sixth day which sees an important innovation; here the account no longer says, "God said," but "God said *to them*" (1:28); the simple pronoun points to God's first interlocutors, man and woman. By speaking to humanity in this way, God is also discreetly offering the possibility of responding, of entering into dialogue. God is also giving humanity the gift of speech to man, and by enabling us to speak within the sanctuary, God is making of people liturgical worshippers. The human person is both the image of God and a worshipper in his presence. The worship thus prepared is to take place in dialogue with God. In this way, from the first moment man addresses God within the sanctuary, our speech is to be prayer, given that every word addressed to God is prayer.

All this is most discreetly introduced by the text: the gift of speech, the invitation to respond in prayer, but it is

5. More literally the meaning here is worshiper. The French reads *liturge* and the passage continues talking about *liturgie*, liturgy. We use the word to indicate a formal, written form of church service; however the author uses it much more generally. In his book *Evening, morning and noon . . .* he speaks of the worship in heaven of Revelation 4 and 5 as "liturgy" and links this worship with our faltering but genuine worship on earth. Thus, our every act of worship is a participation in heavenly liturgy. Here he speaks of Adam becoming, so to speak, a liturgical worshiper. (Trans.)

all no more than suggested. God has no wish to obligate us to pray. Prayer is not a duty but springs out of human liberty; it is entirely free and so can express our free love for God. We are free to take up the opportunity to speak, just as God offers, free to pray, free to love. This is fundamental if prayer is not to lose its essence.

To further emphasize the fact of invitation to prayer rather than imposition, God speaks to his man twice, carefully arranging a silence between the two occasions (1:28 and 29). God speaks to the man a first time, and then is silent. In the silence that follows this first speech, just as in the silence that follows the second, God is surely awaiting a response. He awaits it, but does not require it. The silence is hopeful of a response but is without constraint. There is only the gentle pressure of love, which solicits, invites, respecting the man's liberty.

God is silent, but the continuation of the passage shows that the man did not open his mouth but was mute; he did not pray!

Thus the sixth day drew to a close . . .

God ponders and listens in silence

Then comes the seventh day, a day which is altogether extraordinary in that God created nothing more. Everything had been made, so why then should there be one day more? On this seventh day, God neither created nor said anything else; it's a day marked by the extraordinary feature of God's silence!

Already, during the first six days, God's silence is a very evident fact, much more evident than his word. Thus, on the first day God says only the one thing, "Light be," and this word took immediate effect, "Light was."

Afterwards, the rest of the day is silence, but the quality of the silence is important; it was a contemplative silence. In the silence, in fact, God considered the light: "He saw that the light was good." God silently contemplated the light. The same took place on the following days: God creates by his word and then at length considers each of his creations in silence. Each was good and beautiful in his sight, conformable to his will. Genesis 1 enables us to discover a contemplative God!

When the man and the woman are created, God marvels still more in his contemplative silence: "God saw that it was very good" (1:31).

After speaking to his man, God begins to listen; his marveling silence leads him to listen. This is the silence which marks the seventh day; God ponders and listens to the worshipper to whom he has given the gift of speech. Without God's listening ear, there would be no purpose to prayer.

God "blessed and sanctified" the seventh day (2:3). For no other day did he do this; by blessing and sanctifying this day, God made it a day for a feast. God is quiet: the worship of this feast could now begin in the sanctuary that is the cosmos. In silence, God awaits the prayer of people, but without having made it an obligation. The summit of creation is here, not on the sixth day with the creation of humanity, but on the seventh, the day of God's man in prayer; it's an extraordinary summit, in which it is suggested that we give creation its finishing touches in prayer.

Never had any person responded to God's voice. On this occasion, God speaks and is then silent; finally he is to hear a voice other than his own. God makes his silence a jewel-case in which to enfold man's prayer. It is a silence of infinite love, a love full of hope and confidence. God had neither blessed nor sanctified the days on which he had spoken; he does bless and sanctify the day on which he ceases to speak in order to listen to man. Humbly, God accords greater value to our prayer than to his own speech.

How could there be a more wonderful silence than God's! People today complain that God's silence is heavy to bear, painful to feel. Is there not a misunderstanding here, a mistaking, a confusion? The passage about "the foundation of the world" presents us with a completely different view. God is thirsty for prayer; his silence speaks magnificently of all that he is awaiting from humanity, awaiting in love, hope, confidence, humility . . .

The eternal day

The seventh day had no evening or morning, unlike the six other days of "the world's foundation." When it comes to worship, there is no evening or morning either; we might say that it is an eternal day. In this way we come to see that there are really two ways of understanding time. There is chronological time, made up of evenings and mornings, and liturgical[6] time which has neither evening nor morning. These two aspects of time are not somehow successive but rather superimposed such that time may be experienced in a chronological way or a liturgical way. God himself begins by seeing time chronologically, but then changes from the moment of humanity's creation. Then the evening and morning cease really to be of much importance, so much more important is the encounter of prayer . . . Chronological time is at the margins of eternity, but liturgical time already has the savor of eternity such that

6. Liturgy is seen in, for example, eastern orthodox churches as central to worship and as a participation in heaven and the eternal; see also note 3 above. (Trans.)

today still we belong to the blessed and sanctified seventh day which has no evening or morning. As we encounter God, we enter into God's eternity.

Today again, God silently hopes for and awaits the adoration of his most beautiful creature . . .

What would the prayer of the man be in this sanctified cosmos? In first place it might well be an immense silence, the silence of profound contemplation . . . Once created, man, as he entered this temple, had good reason to ponder deeply the very things God dwelt on so profoundly. This day which opens onto eternity leads to contemplation of all that is on display; the contemplation too concerns eternity.

After a lengthy consideration of every created thing, humanity then has a fullness of time to consider the creator himself. On this day without evening or morning, we have eternity before us to contemplate the one who in love entrusts the whole world to us. If God is contemplative, then the contemplative in us has plenty of material, and in this way too we are in God's image. People and God can therefore have communion in contemplation; and from this communion of love will spring the first words of prayer . . .

Today too, as part of this seventh day which has neither evening nor morning, God thinks on humanity and silently waits . . . .

The prayer of fire

One day a brother came to visit the cell of Abba Arsenius.[7] (We find ourselves in the desert of Scetis in Egypt during the fourth century.) The brother looked through the window and saw Arsenius, his whole being like a fire. The brother was worthy of this vision. When he knocked, the

7. Fr. *Arsène.* (Trans.)

old man came out and saw the brother in a state of astonishment. He said to him, "Have you been at the door for long? Did you see something?" The other replied, "No!" After he had spoken with him, he let him go. (Apophthegm 65).

Arsenius: here we see a man of prayer deep in contemplation of God on this blessed and holy seventh day, which has neither evening nor morning!

Arsenius was "like a fire," it is said. The fire with which Arsenius burned is fire far greater than anything we know. It is a fire that burns without consuming, just as was the fire of God in the burning bush. One would have to be "worthy" to see this, just as the apophthegm says. The brother was worthy of the vision but regarded himself as unworthy to speak of it. God alone can light such a fire; his whole being is fire; and Arsenius, immersed in God, burned with that fire. This is the sort of contemplative prayer that God looks for, a prayer of fire, the prayer of a worshiper immersed in the fire of God's silence.

We all have this experience of God's silence, but not as Arsenius experienced it in prayer; we have difficulty perceiving that this silence is a listening silence. Nevertheless . . .

When somone is listening to us, we do notice it in a certain indefinible way; each of us has the experience of being listened to by someone else or indeed by a whole group of listeners. We realize that someone is listening without being able to say how. We can also sense whether the attention of the listener is slight or intense; and the same is true with God. He listens in silence. We are not always aware of this listening ear, but sometimes an awareness is given us and even the ability to sense the degree of attention with which he is listening. We sense this to a greater or lesser degree, not because God is listening to a varying degree. He is always listening to us with the utmost attention, an attention as deep as his love; but our hearts are more or less sensitive to this love, more or less open to God. Arsenius and Adam were not equally open to God's attentive love.

Adam had perceived nothing of God's attentive listening. He didn't know, and couldn't or didn't wish to respond to God's expectant silence. Already he had begun to turn things over with a serpent![8] Adam had turned his back towards God! He did not pray! He limited himself to speaking about God, forming his theology together with a serpent!

The silence of God becomes a wounded silence . . .

We don't know how to pray

We might know how to talk about God from the word go, but we don't know how to pray! Perhaps this is what the brother thought as he left Arsenius? In any case, it is what I would have thought had I been this brother; will I one day know how to pray?

"We don't know how to pray," we say so often! It is also what Paul wrote to the Romans (8:26), and he noted it with sorrow. What is necessary if we are to learn to pray? What will make us competent? Who will give us the first word, and light in us the fire of prayer?

Paul's answer is clear: the Holy Spirit comes to our help and teaches us to pray by praying with us and in us. Without the Holy Spirit our prayer is unformed and void, an abyss of darkness. Without him, we know nothing of God, nothing of the depths of his silence, of the depths of his listening, the depths of his love . . . Only the Spirit can

8. The idea of Adam being influenced by Satan prior to the critical moment of "the Fall" is far from unusual in the spiritual literature. (Trans.)

ever sound the depths of God. Only the Spirit can bring prayer to birth in us and help us to fulfill each liturgical task, each act of worship, in the temple of the cosmos.

The Holy Spirit for prayer

The creation account tells us that the Spirit was there, present from the beginning! "The Spirit of God hovered over the waters" (Gen 1:2).

The Holy Spirit was there even before God spoke. He precedes the creative word, just as he is there with it and continues with it in silence.

In Gen 1:2 and throughout the narrative, the Holy Spirit is silent. It is the silence from which each creative word springs, as it is the silence from which our prayer can burst forth. The Spirit gives power to each creative word, just as he is able to provide power to our prayer. The Spirit is there, silent, expectant, listening. He waits for us to invoke his help, to provide inspiration to our worship, to birth prayer in us and give it life.

"The Spirit of God hovered over the waters": by using the word "hover," Genesis compares the Holy Spirit to a bird in the sky, above us, and inaccessible.

The verb "hover" is as rare as it is magnificent. The only other passage which uses it of a bird is that in Deut 32:11. There it serves to describe God, comparing him to a hovering eagle. "Hover" describes rather precisely the almost stationary position of a bird which moves no more than the extremities of its wings so as to stay where it is, to hang in the air above whatever has attracted its attention. In this passage, God is not hovering above his prey, but above his little ones. His close attention has nothing menacing about it but is perfectly beneficent, protective. The eagle is attentive to the slightest cry of its chicks, ready to draw near, take them up on its wings and carry them, when they have no idea how to fly.

Such is the Holy Spirit; he hovers in silence above us, beyond our grasp to be sure; but he is waiting for us to call upon him to descend upon us and lead us in prayer. Without him we are incapable of prayer, even though prayer is what we were made for. Our first prayer then should surely be one of invoking the Spirit in one way or another: "Come, Holy Spirit, creator God!" as we sing in the west, or, as in the Eastern church, "Heavenly King, comforter, Spirit of truth, you who are present everywhere, you who fill all things; treasure of goodness and giver of life, come and dwell in us; purify us of every pollution and save us, you who are kind."

In the cosmic sanctuary, the Spirit awaits our prayer in silence, to birth us into prayer and immerse us in the depths of God.

"Lord, open my lips and my mouth shall show forth your praise," as most monks say at the opening of the very first devotions of the day. This prayer may also be addressed to the Spirit; in it we not only ask him to give the first word of prayer but even request that he open our lips in order to pronounce it. By praying like this we accord the Holy Spirit the very first place in our prayer, so that, when we come down to it, the prayer is more his than ours; his, and he makes us a gift of it. In truth, prayer is a work of the Holy Spirit in us.

The fire that took hold of Arsenius is the fire of the Holy Spirit. The same fire took hold of another desert father, Joseph of Panepho; his fingers became lamps of fire when he began to pray (Apoph. 390). The expression "lamps of fire" is taken from the New Testament, where it is found just once, in Rev 4:5, as a designation of the Holy Spirit. This tells us that the fire on Joseph, as with Arsenius, was the fire of the Holy Spirit.

Following a most beautiful patristic image, Joseph and Arsenius burned just as iron burns in a fire. The iron is not the fire, but it becomes fire when it is placed in the fire. It becomes fire while remaining iron.[9] This is how a person can be sanctified by God, transformed into him, even deified[10] by his grace, which is to say, "partaking of the divine nature," as stated in 2 Pet 1:4. Just as iron becomes fire in the fire while remaining iron, so we, as we pray, become divine in God, while remaining human.

The intensity of the fire most often escapes us, but the Spirit comes within us just the same when we call upon him; he abides within, though, at times, as if a feeble and imperceptible flame. What prevents us from perceiving his presence are the other loves that burn within, fires of desires which we at times stir up rather more than the fire of desire for God.

The serpent has found out how to light this fire of desire. Adam responded to that fire rather than to God. Between the serpent and the Spirit who hovered over him, Adam chose the serpent, so wounding God in his silence. The silence of the seventh day became a wounded silence, as seen in its extreme form on the seventh day of holy week; between the Friday of the cross and the Sunday of resurrection, the deep silence of that holy Saturday veils the unspeakable wounding to God's heart.

9. In the French there is a nice play on words; iron is *fer*, while fire is *feu*; thus *fer* becomes *feu*. (Trans.)

10. This term, while somewhat alien to western thinking, is a commonplace of Orthodox theology. (Trans.)

A man at last meets God's expectation

Just as Adam, and everyone in him, unfailingly wounds God in his longing over us, so too God unfailingly continues to hope. Since that first morning, the Spirit has not ceased to hover over the waters, waiting for a man worthy of the name to step forth out of the waters, that he might come to rest upon him, upon a man who is turned towards him, not responding in the slightest degree to the solicitations of the serpent.

In the silence of God, in the silence of the Holy Spirit, there is a man who came up out of the water, under the vault of heaven in the sanctuary of the cosmos, from the waves of Jordan. As he came out of the water, his speech was not addressed to the crowd; "he prayed," Luke states (3:21); he perfectly met the expectation of God . . . At last! Then the Holy Spirit descended upon him; the heavens were opened and God in his contemplation abandoned his silence and marveled, "You are my beloved Son; I have placed all my affection upon you."

On this blessed and sanctified day, a day without end, one that has neither evening nor morning, Christ's prayer fulfilled the longings of the Father and of the Spirit in this cosmic sanctuary. Christ is the perfect worshiper, whose prayer completes creation. Entirely in God in his prayer, he is enveloped in fire, as became apparent to those who were worthy of the vision on the mount of transfiguration.

"Father," he said in his final prayer, "as you have sent me into this sanctuary that is the world, I now send them."

Without staff or sandals

Despite the Fall, the cosmos is always a holy place, as God himself recalls by the mouth of the prophet: "Heaven is my throne and earth is my footstool" (Isa 66:1). This view of the world is also the view of Jesus, who likewise saw heaven as God's throne and the earth as his footstool (Matt 5:34–35).

As a demonstration to his people that the ground they occupied was always holy, God sent one of his servants to Joshua, shortly after Israel had crossed the Jordan: "Remove the sandals from your feet; the place where you are standing is holy" (Josh 5:15). This remains the custom in the near East; in a sanctuary the feet are to be bare (see Exod 3:5).

When Jesus sent his disciples out, the instructions accompanying their sending vary somewhat according to which gospel you read. It is interesting to note that in Matthew, Jesus requires the disciples to go "without staff or sandals" (10:10), which corresponds exactly to the behavior to be adopted in the Temple or synagogues. By forbidding staff and sandals in this way, Jesus demonstrated that he considers the earth into which he sends disciples a holy place.

Returning now to the high priestly prayer, we have seen that when Jesus speaks of "the foundation of the world," we need to think in terms of a cosmic temple.

In this prayer, when Jesus refers to all he has been through during his time on this earth, he speaks of it in a significant way: "I have glorified you in the earth," he says in 17:4. In speaking like this, we see Jesus viewing his life as worship to the glory of God, and himself as a worshiper. "I have glorified you in the earth": if in this great temple of the world God had been awaiting the worship of men, here, his desire was now fulfilled; Christ acts as a worshiper, affirming what the angels say in heaven: "Holy, holy, holy is the Lord; the whole earth is full of his glory" (Isa 6:3).

"I have made manifest your name," Jesus adds (17:6), which is to say, "I have revealed your name." In Israel, the manifestation of God's name was only to take place in one particular place, in the most holy place of the sanctuary, and it pertained to the high priest alone to reveal this unspeakable name to others. By manifesting the name of God, Jesus was acting as a high priest in a temple, the temple of the cosmos. His very life, his entire life is a revelation of the unspeakable name; his life is a liturgy of the ineffable, apophatic[11] prayer, as theologians would say. Jesus is also the one who manifests the being of God, who makes God visible; "He who has seen me has seen the Father"; in this way he is the perfect image of the Father, within the cosmic temple.

After being sanctified and sent into the world (10:36), Jesus now sends his disciples to, in their turn, engage with his mission; that is, to glorify God in the earth and manifest his name. When Jesus asks God to sanctify the disciples, the purpose is to send them too as worshipers into the holy place, that they might participate in the cosmic celebration that has neither evening nor morning.

Now that the Son has interceded with the Father, the disciples can have their prayers rise up to God within this cosmic temple, thereby honoring the world which since its "foundation" had been created to celebrate God's glory.

Without either staff or sandals, the disciple is to be what he or she was created for, a being of prayer, standing before God, with the Son and in the Spirit, a being of fire, in God.

---

11. Reproducing the French *apophatique*, forming a word that does not actually exist in English dictionaries. *Apophasis* is a figure of speech in which you allude to something by denying that you intend to talk about it. (Trans.)

Certainly the world has been mismanaged by man; it is polluted, profaned, transformed into a den of thieves, a "house of merchandise"[12] and even a battlefield . . . , but this doesn't stop it from having left God's hands as a holy place, which Jesus, like God, considers always as a sanctuary, in which it is good to walk reverently, barefoot, without sandals or staff, in praise.

"Holy Father, sanctify them as I send them into this holy place which is the world"; sanctify them, just as you sanctify this earth by your presence alone; sanctify them, just as you have sanctified this day without evening or morning, that they might accomplish before you their office of worship.[13] Sanctify them as you are holy, making them beneficiaries of the holiness which you offer them. Sanctify them, by saying to them in blessing, "Be holy for I am holy; my holy blessing now makes you holy"; and may this blessing also be an invitation which they can freely accept or decline; "I am holy, therefore be holy too, though you may refuse to be so."

Our presence in the sanctuary

Reader friend, if Jesus, then, is sending us into the world as into a sanctuary, a holy place, his commission mobilizes us in a very particular way.

A sanctuary does not belong to the worshipers who assemble there but to the God who is worshiped. It is not a property of men but of God. If the world is a sanctuary, we should comport ourselves as God's guests. This leads to reflection on the way we manage this earth, misuse it, pollute it, transform it into a den of thieves. This goes beyond the

12. John 2:16
13. Literally, "their liturgical office." (Trans.)

simple issue of ecology, which deals with managing things for the common good and the welfare of future generations. It concerns so much more; it means managing and looking after things not for our good, but for God's.

If we are not in our own home on this earth, not even when we are in our houses, then in every place we should be conducting ourselves as one does in a sanctuary, paying intense attention to the presence of God, humbly conscious of our unworthiness to stand before God, and with overflowing thanksgiving to know ourselves received by the one who created this earth with a view to meeting with us.

Since we are in the world as in a temple, our sight should be fixed with attention on the only representative figure to be found there, the only image, the human being. We are called upon to consider others as being images of God, gods under God, according to the beautiful patristic formulation! (see Ps 82:6) For sure, in every human person, the image of God is unhappily marred, but it is intact and perfect in Jesus (2 Cor 4:4, Col 1:15). Through the outlook formed as we contemplate Christ, we can rediscover in each person the still present image of God, the being of prayer each one is called to become in God's sight. Christ teaches us to view others as beloved images of God, as beings called to be face to face with him in prayer; he sends us out alongside them to love them with his love: "As I have loved you, you are to love each other," he says to his disciples (John 15:12) before he sends them into this world's sanctuary.

Going into the world as into a sanctuary also means treating all things as not belonging to us, including our own assets. Everything is God's, down to the last dish, the smallest object; everything should be used as though it were furniture in the Jerusalem Temple, with the greatest of care, the greatest veneration, but without any idolizing either.

No more than in a sanctuary should anything on this earth be wasted, not even a crust of bread. On every occasion Jesus is seen with bread in his hands, he gives thanks to God. After he satisfies the crowds he makes sure that all that is left is gathered up into baskets, just as everything in the Temple that could nourish was handled with great care. Not only is the immense wastage of our rich countries an offense with respect to poor countries, but it is also an offence before the one who provides us with so very much.

Each situation, each event in our lives, each of our actions is to be viewed through the perspective of worship, of liturgy, as is everything that takes place in a temple; which is to say that we can pass through every situation accompanying it with a prayer of thanksgiving, of repentance, of intercession or consecration, according to the case. There can be no exception. In a temple, everything finds its truth and real depth in God. Thus it is with everything that makes up our life once we remember that this world is a sanctuary.

Barefooted on this earth, as were the disciples sent by Jesus into the sanctuary of the cosmos, it may be that we discover to our shame the dirtiness of our feet! Welcomed by God himself into his temple, we are overwhelmed with emotion by the unprecedented gesture of the one who receives us; he takes a cloth, binds it around his waist, and begins to wash our feet . . . this is how God himself welcomes his guests into his temple!

"O Lord our God, how majestic is your name throughout the universe!

When I consider the heavens, the works of your hands,

The moon and the stars which you have ordained . . .

What is man that you should think on him . . . ?"
(Ps 8)

The interior sanctuary

It would be incomplete were we to pass over in silence what the high priestly prayer says concerning another sanctuary, one to which Jesus similarly alludes, and which makes still more precious all we have said about the sanctuary of the cosmos. In fact, Jesus considers each disciple to be a sanctuary, not simply as being an image of God or as a worshiper in the cosmic temple, but as forming a sanctuary in him or herself.

"Father," says Jesus, "may I be in them and you in me" (17:23). Praying like this, asking his Father to be present with him in the disciples, Jesus regards each of them as a place in which God can be, and so, as a sanctuary.

"Sanctify them"; this request of Jesus thus takes on a new significance: sanctify them as you would sanctify a sanctuary by your presence within it. The presence of the Father and of the Son, along with the Spirit, this is what sanctifies us: "We will come to him and will take up residence in him" (John 14:23).

The disciple as a sanctuary; this is the astonishing perspective that the priestly prayer now opens up, plunging us into new depths of meditation!

"I in them, and you in me"; when is this prayer of Christ's to be fulfilled? When we truly become God's dwelling place? By faith, Paul tells us, it is already the case. "The temple of God is holy, which temple you are" (1 Cor 3:17); "we are the temple of the living God" (2 Cor 6:16).

If our whole being is a temple of God, it follows that we no longer belong to ourselves. We are God's. We can no longer do just any old thing with our bodies, with our lives. Our body and life are not to be ridiculed nor made subject to idolatry, but honored as a place in which God is present to meet with us.

The same applies to other people; they too are sanctuaries, so that we should have for each of them the respect and veneration due to every place where God is. It would be well if we were to bow down before every person we meet.

Let us be quiet, reader friend, as quiet as a holy place which fills with silence when God is present.

Let us be quiet, because Jesus, who had nowhere to lay his head, has asked his Father to make his dwelling place within us; let us be still, because he has now found in us the place of his rest.

Let us be quiet, because his presence in us already sanctifies us. "I sanctify myself for them, that they too may be sanctified" (John 17:19).

Let us be quiet, because, with the Son, the Spirit too comes to take up residence within us (1 Cor 3:16, 6:19).

Let us be quiet, to listen deep within, in the holy of holies, to the one who comes to pronounce the name of the Father, saying "Abba," as in a whisper, a murmur of silence . . .

Indeed, let us observe silence . . .

Then, when in your silence the blessed name resounds, bow down in the presence of the one who fills the sanctuary with his glory.

Holy, holy, holy is the Lord!

Heaven and earth are full of his glory!

3

THE WORLD AS
BATTLEFIELD

While the world is a sanctuary in Christ's eyes, in the eyes of God, and, it is to be hoped, in our eyes, it also at the same time has for Jesus a quite different reality to it, altogether negative and at the other extreme. This is what we now need to talk about, without ever forgetting the holiness of the cosmos, a fact Jesus never lost from view.

The double reality of this world

If we take a quick look at the different uses of the word "world" in John's Gospel, we very soon discover this double reality, a reality at once eminently positive but also simply negative. "The world was made by the light," verse 10 of the prologue tells us very positively, but continues immediately with the desolate "but the world knew him not."

"God so loved the world that he gave his only Son" (3:16); this expression locates the world in the wonderfully high place of being loved. "So" is a superlative which magnificently underlines the love of God for his creation. However, faced with this extreme love of God, the world reacts with hatred towards the only Son! The world meets the love with hatred! "It has hated me without cause," Jesus deplores (15:25).

This hatred felt by the world towards the Son does not prevent him from loving it to the point of coming to take upon himself the sin of the world (1:29); the works of the world are indeed evil (7:7). Jesus comes to give his life for the world (6:33), to save it (3:17). This does not, however, cause the hatred of the world for Jesus to disappear, and it even extends to include the disciples (15:18).

From this hatred that comes from the world, a state of conflict is born, such that Jesus speaks of himself as "persecuted," and warns the disciples that the same will be true for them (15:20). Jesus, though, takes care to reassure his disciples, and informs them of the result of the struggle: "Fear not, I have overcome the world" (16:33).

"I have overcome the world." This statement shows the extent to which the world has become an enemy, despite the great love of God for it. What an astonishing and disappointing world, capable of such enmity towards the very one who loves it to the very highest degree.

This, then, is the double reality of the world in Jesus' eyes and the eyes of God: the object of an infinite love and the subject of an unbelievable hatred.

The warfare context of the priestly prayer

"I have overcome the world." Jesus' statement is well-known, but it is not often realized that we are dealing here with the last words Jesus addressed to his disciples, the very last words before the high priestly prayer. It is immediately after he has affirmed his victory over the enemy that Jesus begins to prayer, which situates the high priestly prayer against a backdrop which is simply one of war.

When Jesus opens his prayer for his disciples who he sends into the world, it is not in a setting of peace finally recovered, but of continuing conflict, because, despite the victory of Christ, the hatred of the world has not disappeared.

When, prior to the prayer, Jesus had hidden nothing of his victory from his disciples, neither did he hide anything of what would happen to them: "You will know the oppression of the world" (16:33). "You are not of the world, which is why the world hates you" (15:19).

It's in this climate of hatred that Jesus sends his disciples into the world; it is how he sends us too! It is so necessary that he pray for us!

All this calls us to return to our reading of the high priestly prayer, but now from a different angle. Before doing so, there is a hidden reef which we need immediately to point out; we don't wish to be dashed against the rocks of what is usually termed the Manichean error.

The Manichean error

The Manichean movement was born with Manes early in the third century and deeply marked the history of the Church at that period. The Manicheans were great readers of John's Gospel, but only understood from it one aspect of the world, the negative. They forgot that the world is good, and they wound up saying not only that the "works of the world are evil," but that the world itself is evil. Never, though, in John or indeed anywhere in the Bible is it said that the world is bad. The Manicheans forgot the way God looked at the world at first: "God saw all that he had made, and, behold, it was very good" (Gen 1:31).

The way the Manicheans saw the world was a caricature; they forgot the positive and remembered only the negative.

Opposed to modern day Manichean ideas, and they are still around, there are others, just as extreme but at the opposite end of the scale, for whom the world is good, purely good, thereby positing man as in an edenic, idyllic relationship with the creation. Everything is harmonious, peaceable, to the point of ignoring the belligerent context of which Jesus spoke to his disciples before sending them into the midst of the world.

The true enemy

In order not to fall into the Manichean error, we will endeavor to point out the true nature of the adversary Jesus is thinking of when he says "I have overcome the world."'

Where the Manicheans were mistaken about the nature of the world, it is because they didn't see the elision taking place in the statement "I have overcome the world"; it needs to be understood more precisely as "I have overcome the prince of the world."

In fact it is not the world, properly speaking, which is the enemy of Christ since this world is loved by God. No! The real enemy is "the prince of the world," as Jesus said, designating Satan (12:31). It is he, Satan, who has subjected the world to himself, causing it to share in his hatred for Christ. Satan is a usurper who has seduced the world and manipulates it by turning it against Christ and his disciples. When Christ reveals himself as victor over the world, this above all means saving the world from Satan's schemes. This is why Jesus can say at one and the same time that he is victor over and savior of the world.

The abbreviation of "I have overcome the prince of the world" into "I have overcome the world" is clearly noted by John, as we see in his first epistle. The apostle, in fact, begins by speaking unequivocally of "victory over the Evil One" (1 John 2:13, 14), before speaking with more concision of "victory over the world" (1 John 5:4).

By confounding the devil with the world, the Manicheans demonize the world, something Jesus never did. Once we have discarded this confusion, we can understand without any difficulty Jesus' request of his Father in his high priestly prayer: "I am not asking that they be taken out of the world, but that they be preserved from the Evil One" (17:15). The world is always a sanctuary, a holy place. With Jesus there is nothing of the sadist who would send his disciples into the maw of the wolf! He sends them where they can celebrate God, but also into a place where the enemy holds sway, but an enemy who can be resisted with the help Jesus asked of his Father: "Keep them from the Evil One."

Being and becoming

If the true enemy is Satan, then the world becomes more precisely the prize of the conflict between Christ and Satan, and the scene of that conflict. Thus it is that the world is a battlefield on which the disciples in their turn will know their fill of tribulations.

In the end, then, in Jesus' eyes the world is both a holy place and a field of battle. This twin reality needs to be borne constantly in mind, without forgetting the essential specific that the world is above all and fundamentally a holy place, and that it has only subsequently become a battlefield. The negative reality is secondary; it is a temporary manifestation within history, a problematic but passing degradation which does not compromise the primary reality, which endures despite everything.

In short, the world is a holy place; it has certainly become a battlefield, but despite that remains a sanctuary. There is nothing in the Bible that would allow us to think otherwise, to think that the world is firstly a battlefield, an enemy territory to be conquered and transformed into a place of safety. No! The Bible clearly affirms that the world is above all a holy place, but nevertheless a sanctuary to be restored given that it has become a theatre of war.

The merchants in the Temple

To help us clearly perceive the twin reality of the world, John's Gospel places at the outset of Jesus' ministry an episode which particularly clearly demonstrates the whole nature of what he was doing. Jesus enters the Temple in Jerusalem and sets to chasing out the merchants. It's very clear; the Temple is the particular sanctuary of God; it is "the house of my Father," Jesus says (2:16). However, the merchants have made it "a house of merchandise" (2:16). The battlefield aspect is apparent when Jesus arms himself with a whip to fight with those who are usurpers. The Temple is at all times the house of God; Jesus therefore fights to reestablish this profound reality, driving out the undesirable usurpers. It is just the same with the world; it is at all times the house of God; its owner is at all times God, not the Evil One, who is an undesirable usurper, a "squatter" on what is still God's property.

The other Gospels function in more of a historical mode by placing this scene at the close of Jesus' ministry. John places it at the outset a in highly significant way, shedding light on the ministry as a whole, helping us understand the way the world is similar to the temple;

it remains a holy place, though at this present time it has become a battlefield.

Sanctify them

Before sending his disciples into the world, Jesus asks his Father to sanctify them. We can now advance rather further into an understanding of this request. If the world is a battlefield, why now ask for the sanctification of the disciples? This all becomes clear when we refer back to the vocabulary of warfare in the Old Testament.

In itself war is a calamity; this must never cease to be said! Nevertheless, the Bible, does speak, in a positive way, of "the wars of the Lord" (1 Sam 25:28). God is frequently termed "the Lord of the armies"; he is also described as a military chief who leads his armies into battle (Ex 15:4; Ps 18 . . .). If he, the Holy One, throws himself into a war, this war, led by the Holy God, must logically be considered a "holy war" since everything undertaken by God is holy.

I am aware that this way of speaking can be rather uncomfortable at a time when for certain islamist extremists a supposedly holy war is again the order of the day, but such extremists have nothing to do with the Bible and ought not to affect a biblical outlook. (I believe that their reading of the Koran is erroneous, but I leave that debate to muslims; my concern is the Bible.) However, the history of the Church does reveals the same misunderstandings; the crusades and other wars in the name of God are unquestionable proof. This doesn't make it any the less true that there are ambiguous texts in the Bible and so the misunderstanding needs to be corrected.

What exactly is the (genuine) holy war? For a Christian, it seems to me, the only way to understand things is to turn to Christ, who will bring light to this difficult question.

The only holy war, if there is such a thing, is the war to which Jesus alluded when he said "I have overcome the world." The only war in which Jesus participated was the one that made him the conqueror of the world. This war, looked at globally, is the only "holy war" we can envisage in a positive way. This certainly concerns us in so far as Jesus warns his disciples that they will meet with hatred and tribulations in this world. We are thrust into the heart of conflict.

The sanctification of soldiers

We return to the biblical language of the holy war. Every war fought by God is holy; but more, all who fight under God's leadership must also be considered holy. To participate in God's work, one would have to be holy as he is, sanctified by him. This is why, in the Old Testament, all who fought in a holy war had first to be sanctified.

"Sanctify yourselves for war" is stated in both Joel (3:9) and Jeremiah (6:4). These requirements spoken to the people come from God. The prophets are not speaking of just any war but only war directed by God, so we see why the soldiers, who fight alongside God, are said to be "sanctified" in Isaiah 13:3; they were sanctified in order to participate in the holy war under the command of the holy God.

If we maintain the spirit of this ancient biblical practice, the issue becomes clear. "Sanctify them," Jesus asks of his Father; this request sees the disciples as soldiers who are to be sent into the battle ground of the world.

What exactly is this holy war?

The war for truth

"Sanctify them by the truth; your word is truth" (17:17); these are the exact terms in which Jesus requests sanctification. It is the whole of this phrase that we need to understand if we are not to mistake the war, and not enlist God in support of our own barbaric actions.

"Sanctify them by the truth; your word is truth." According to Jesus' request, it is by his word that God sanctifies, and this quite simply, it seems to me, is because the conflict is situated precisely at the level of words.

If the word of God is termed truth, if it is assimilated to the truth, this would imply that there is also a word of untruth, of lies, and this enables us to identify the enemy — the adversary is the lie. Thus the holy war is seen to be between the lie and the truth. This is apparent in a very clear way in John's Gospel.

From the opening of his Gospel, John speaks of "the word," placing it alongside God because it is God (1:1); he presents it as incarnate in Christ (1:14), so much so that it can be said that Jesus is the Word of God. Furthermore, in this same Gospel, Jesus presents himself as being "the truth" (14:6), so that indeed to be sanctified by the truth or by the word is to be sanctified by Christ; it is to participate in the life of Christ, and so, also, in his struggle.

Opposed to Christ we find Satan, who is designated by Jesus quite simply and in a most suggestive way as "the father of lies" (8:44). The holy war is therefore the conflict between Jesus and Satan, which is to say between the truth and the lie, or again, staying with John's terminology, the conflict between light and darkness. It is a war which is situated at the level of words, not at the level of armaments as used by men in their military conflicts. It has nothing to do with wars, even those we may say are "just."

The war is the one Jesus leads against the lie, which also means against the half-truth, the slander, against calumny and defamation, against words of hatred, anger, jealousy, prideful words, words that discourage, that wound, that murder, that bring despair, as too, words that flatter and seduce, words that misinform, hypocritical words. The adversary, the lie, in all its forms, is so very prevalent today. When Jesus tells his disciples that they will experience oppression in the world, he is speaking of the oppression of the lie, and this is exactly our continuing experience.

The war is all too real. It is a genuine war which causes millions of victims around us and amongst us. This is what you are going to have to suffer, Jesus tells us. This is the combat for which he is preparing us when he asks the Father for our sanctification.

To face up to such a war means finding ourselves in situations in which the word has been muzzled, heavily criticized, repressed, bullied into submission, enclosed within an imprisoning silence which has nothing to do with the silence of adoration that permeates the sanctuary.

Such tribulations you are going to know, Jesus tells us, and you will discover numbers of victims around you and among you.

Before we head into combat as we follow Christ, we need to examine just how he himself fought the father of lies.

Christ's struggle

"I have overcome the world": when Jesus says this, the hour of his passion has yet to come; the cross is still a prospect, albeit in the near future. Nevertheless, Jesus speaks as of the past: "I have overcome." We normally see Jesus' victory as taking place on the cross, which is true; the cross is Christ's victory. But by speaking here of the past, Jesus draws his disciples' attention to those things prior to the cross which already speak of his victory. The cross is the victory in that it is the final blow delivered to the enemy. "I have overcome the world"; by speaking in this way Jesus invites us to see the whole of his life as a battle. Was there some one precise moment prior to the cross which might constitute the definitive victory? I think not! I believe rather that each moment of Jesus' life is to be seen as victorious.

One might think that Jesus' victory is most particularly at the moment of the temptation in the wilderness after the 40 days of struggle; but John's Gospel does not report this episode.

No single passage in this Gospel specifies Jesus' victory; I believe there are two reasons.

First of all, because the victory is, in a way, beyond description; it is located at such depth or at such a height of spiritual reality that we need to content ourselves simply with the encompassing affirmation of Jesus, "I have overcome the world."

In Revelation, in which the vocabulary is not the same as the Gospel, John is able to describe the hidden reality of the holy war. The tone is set in the first description of Christ; he appears with "a sharp two-edged sword coming out of his mouth" (1:16). This very suggestive image is of Jesus as a warrior, and locates the combat decidedly at the level of words, speech, and there alone; this sword is the only weapon borne by Christ, and reappears throughout the book. With it Christ "makes war" (2:16). With it he "strikes" the nations (19:15) and "slays" (19:21). The Revelation reveals ("apocalypse" = revelation) the hidden face of the Gospel and demonstrates how indeed the battle with the word is truly a war, a war on the battlefield that is the world.

When the Gospel does describe some one victory of Jesus, this is also because his whole ministry was one long victory, a series of victories. Each episode of his life is a victory over the world. Some examples will show this.

From the beginning

"The devil is a murderer from the beginning" (John 8:44). These words of Jesus show that the adversary has held sway "from the beginning," which is to say, since the time of creation.

If the devil is a murderer from the beginning, he must have been confronted from the beginning with the Word, given that John tells us that "in the beginning was the Word." The devil, the murderer, spreads death, but in the Word there is life (1:4). In the Word there is light too (1:4), and the darkness has not been able to overpower it (1:5).

Starting with the Prologue, John presents the Word as unmoved by the darkness of the lie. The darkness could not overpower it. Our modern translations fail to bring out the warlike dimension of this verb "overpower"; they opt instead for a more intellectual translation — "the darkness did not apprehend14 it." The Fathers, however, aware of the primary sense of the verb used, used "overpower," and so made the two great warrior affirmations of the Gospel a magnificent setting for the ministry of Jesus as a whole; the one who from the beginning was not "overpowered" by the darkness could finally affirm with complete truth, "I have overcome the world."

14. The English from the RV; the French here contrasts *soumettre* (bring into submission) with *comprendre* (to understand). (Trans.)

The struggle with the tempter

In the first three Gospels, the great conflict with the devil is described in the account of the temptation. What we should grasp is that this is located right at the start of Jesus' ministry and so, in a sense, "from the beginning". Further, it took place entirely at the level of speech. It was a conflict of words and words alone; the word of truth against the lie. This is the nature of the holy war, this real war which still inflicts its ravages on the battlefield of the world. Jesus victoriously resisted three verbal trials, that is, three assaults of the adversary. Against each word intended to destroy, Jesus found the right answer and prevailed through the word of truth; each word of truth was taken from the Scriptures and is a word of God.

During this conflict in the wilderness, Satan attacked Jesus so perfidiously that he even himself cited the Scriptures (Luke 4:10), the word of God! Satan took a word of truth to make it a word that murders! How foul is this enemy to pervert the Word and make it a lie! Jesus, though, resisted; "full of the Holy Spirit," the Son thrust back by quoting the Father. It is in this Trinitarian communion, in the cohesion of the Son and the Spirit around the word of the Father that victory over the enemy is to be found.

This battle makes us aware that we too could at times be tools of Satan by quoting the word of God! This can happen in theological quarrels when biblical verses are thrown around! Christ was victorious by being humble; he did not push himself forward but simply effaced himself behind a word from his Father, while trusting the Holy Spirit.

The universal character of the temptation account is underlined in Mark's Gospel by the mention of the beasts of the earth and the angels from heaven (1:13). In these created beings, both heaven and earth were witnesses of a battle which escaped human sight.

In Luke's Gospel, the episode concludes with the words, "After tempting him in all these ways, the devil left him for a more favorable time" (4:13). According to Luke, the matter was not closed! The "favorable moment" for a new temptation is in fact described by Luke in the episode of Gethsemane on the Mount of Olives. Jesus' experience here is termed by Luke a "struggle" (which is the primary sense of the word "agony" of 22:44). The struggle was so great that Jesus sweat blood. On this occasion the adversary's weapon was not words but silence. Satan kept quiet the better to hide himself in the night, and it was his silence that assailed Christ. Reader friend, silence at times is the enemy's weapon; it is a crushing silence which has even led to death! In fact every silent falsehood is a weapon of the enemy, and we well know how at times silence can be the silence of deceit.

Jesus' weapon against this deceitful silence was prayer. On the Mount of Olives, Jesus prayed unceasingly; he was then strengthened by an angel, a silent angel, which is to say an angel bearing the silence of the Father and of the Holy Spirit. Reader friend, silence is also a comfort from God when it is freighted with the animating presence of the God who listens and sustains. In his prayer, Jesus leant humbly and with all his strength on the one who infused comfort in the midst of silence: "Your will be done and not mine." In this abandonment to the Father, Jesus was victorious.

All the other struggles

Not only did Jesus vanquish the prince of the world in the desert and on the Mount of Olives, but it's also true of each moment of his ministry. Jesus never ceased to fight; his whole life was combat. He, the non-violent without equal, never failed to pursue this holy war with majestic power. "I have overcome the world" is the final appraisal of his life. It would take too long to go over the whole of Jesus' ministry; I will confine myself to a few points which show the way Jesus never quit the battle at the level of words.

In many gospel passages, various people sought to "test" Jesus, according to some translations, or "lay a trap" for him in others. The Greek verb can also be translated as "tempt." Used in connection with Satan in the wilderness, the verb therefore shows that it was Satan working through those who sought to trap Jesus, interrogating him, for example, about the tribute to be paid Caesar (Matt 22:18), about the great commandment (Mark 22:35), or the case of the woman taken in adultery (John 8:6). We see that in each case the trap was set in the form of verbal dissembling, and that again it was with his word that Jesus gained the victory. He brought to light the trap hidden in an apparently reasonable saying. Satan himself was lurking behind Jesus' interlocutors, but the Truth unmasked the father of lies and manifested his victory by a word of light.

On a number of further occasions, Jesus dealt with hypocrites, unmasking them and exposing the hypocrisy verbally. Hypocrisy takes the form of truth but the lie is lurking behind it. There are hypocritical words just as there are hypocritical silences, and it was always with words that Jesus fought back. Hypocrisy can, like temptation, be deadly and has the devil for its father. Thus, one day Jesus targeted a particular group of hypocrites who by their teaching "tie heavy, crushing burdens and lay them on the shoulders of men" (Matt 23:4). Such burdens have many victims.

Where the father of lies inspires this two-faced teaching, Jesus, by his word, comforts the discouraged (Mt 11:28), quenches the thirsty (John 4:15), redresses, illumines, vivifies, liberates . . . By his teaching, Jesus sanctifies his disciples to help them in their daily struggle.

In this holy war, Jesus also brings victories by setting free the word that has been humiliated, muzzled, repressed, forbidden and silenced . . . By its presence alone, so often, the Word of truth, the incarnate Word can bring truth to others. We see this for example in the meeting between Jesus and blind Bartimaeus. All his life, this man had sought alms from passers-by, and obtained enough to live by from them. In Jesus' presence he asked for something quite different, something he had never had before, the expectation of which had been buried deep in his heart. As he stood before Bartimaeus, Jesus spoke this liberating word, "What do you want me to do for you?" (Luke 18.41). With this question Jesus finally loosed the previously unspoken word which was nonetheless the man's deepest truth, "Lord, that I may receive my sight!" From the depths of darkness in this man, Jesus caused a word of light to spring forth; this word was a prayer, a prayer never before uttered: "Lord, that I may receive my sight!" When God passes by, truth emerges in prayer! It's a great victory over evil when a man is awakened to prayer, as much a victory as the actual fulfillment of prayer. And then, by his sovereign word Jesus did fulfill Bartimaeus' prayer: "Receive your sight; your faith has saved you" (18:42).

Among the many healings wrought by Jesus he brought speech to mutes (Mt 15:30–31), but the same victory of the word of truth over mutism can also be seen in the passages about the healing of lepers. At the time, lepers were condemned to complete exclusion, and so had no access to truth; the healing of a leper meant giving him back the possibility of speech, of communication with those who were well; once cleansed, he could again go to the Temple to pray.

The life of Jesus was so immersed in a conflicted universe that even at his birth, king Herod's sword was unsheathed to kill him (Matt 2:16). By contrast, when Jesus said that he himself was come to bring a sword and not peace (Matt 10:34), he didn't have the same sword in mind; Christ's sword, once again, is his word.

Before sending his disciples into a world which would hate them and in which they would know tribulations, before sending them into this field of battle, Jesus therefore asked his Father to prepare them for this same verbal conflict: "Father, sanctify them by the truth; your word is truth."

A holy disciple

A disciple of Christ, one whom God has sanctified and is therefore holy, not a person sanctified by their own means but one who is holy through God's grace, such a person is one whose speech is fundamentally true; they are without hypocrisy, they speak and live by the word of truth, and bring this truth home to others; their speech is a vehicle for God's word. Holiness like this is urgently needed; we must offer ourselves to live in such a way, since the world is so cunningly manipulated by the father of lies.

A saint is one who applies him or herself to the succor of this world's wounded, those who are bruised, those internally just broken down by untruth, judgments and other words of deceit. The saint draws alongside those who have become silent before men and even before God, and applies

69

themselves to re-establishing in them the word of truth and true prayer.

The saint is listening with such attention that we feel that God himself is listening through them. God alone could give such a quality of listening. The saint reaches the point of understanding the meaning of a silence.

The saint is a person whose presence invites prayer because we sense that they are nothing but prayer and that everything they hear is turned into prayer. The saint's prayer produces a thirst for prayer and brings prayer to birth.

The saint is one whose word is so true that we feel it comes from God. Also, though, such a person is a being of silence who has learned and continually applies themselves to bringing every false inner word to silence. They are a person who maintains silence so as to be impregnated with the word of God and to live by it alone. It is because they know how to listen to God that they know how to listen to others. Their silence brings to birth in others the truth that lies dormant within them.

The holy person in their silence becomes attractive because they are at peace; the peace received from God attracts those whose ability to speak is so bruised.

At the heart of conflict, the saint always considers the world a holy place. Their unceasing prayer rises from the battlefield with great perseverance. Their presence alone reminds men and women that God has not forgotten his sanctuary.

God in his grace gives each age the saints the world needs. Today too he gives us saints along the lines I have been describing, and this is an immense blessing for our times. I think for sure of Seraphim of Sarov, who is well known, a saint whom God had so brought to peace that he became a man of silence, of listening and of truth.

Some years ago, the Lord filled me with joy by enabling me to meet a saint of a similar quality of soul, Father Cleopas. God had quietened, brought peace to this man through long years of silence in a hermitage hidden away in a forest among the Carpathian mountains of Moldavia. Father Cleopas had been there ten years during the communist era, sought by the police and condemned to death. He had prayed for his people throughout those years and God had sanctified him to fight the lie. When he came out of the forest, his sanctified silence attracted people by the thousand. Every day people came to cast before him their burdens, their pains, their damaged reasonings;[15] he would share with them a word of light, a word of truth. I speak of him in the past, because he is now dwelling in the light.

Degrees of struggle

Not all disciples are able to sustain the same struggles. There are degrees of combat, degrees according to which disciples are more or less sanctified. We find the idea that sanctification is a becoming, a process, as stated in Revelation: "let him that is holy be more holy still" (22:11).

In this process of progressive sanctification, the Fathers discerned three stages and established three methods of warfare according to these stages.

The first stage is the beginner stage; this is a saint whose sole tactic is to unceasingly seek refuge in God. Beginners do not apply themselves to fighting as such but to seeking help from God. In this way they are strengthened and others find strength in them too. Don't think that is something

---

15. Literally "wounded words," *paroles blessées*. (Trans.)

71

negligible; far from it! Beginners disconcert the adversary by their constancy in God.

The following stage is the intermediate, the person who is making progress; this is someone who, while relying unceasingly on God, fights the adversary with the weapons the apostle Paul speaks about in Ephesians. It's to those who are well on the way that Paul is speaking in his description of the holy war (6:10–18).

The final stage belongs to the perfect; such a one is so much in Christ that Christ fights in them. They give the world what they have received from God, peace. They bring peace wherever they go.

The daily struggle

Reader friend, the holy war begins today right at our very door, on the threshold of our lips; there we combat everything which belongs to the lie or the half-truth. Our job is to watch over our own tongues, which so easily slip into flattery or judgment, seduction or denigration, and this all the more easily as we find ourselves trusting in a culture which freely uses all these forms of speech . . . how easy it is to howl with the wolves!

We also need to watch over our silences so that they are not silences that put down or crush, but silences that welcome, respect, inspire trust, listen . . .

It is also our place to ask God without ceasing that we be sanctified by him and be bearers of his word of truth.

Equally, we should seek to correct every misunderstanding, to restore truth on every occasion this is possible and useful.

Our place is to use every encounter as an occasion to bring the word of truth, with all the care this requires.

Our place is to struggle amongst those around us against all those mute silences so often unsuspected but which can be so deadly. For example, today there is the frequent issue of rape or incest long buried in silence but which surfaces into speech when the suffering becomes unbearable, when finally the sufferer encounters an ear that will understand.

It is also our place to fight against falsifications of the word of God and their evil results which work away as a hidden poison.

Our place is to watch over the emergence of prayer in another's life and to see it grow into the word of truth, freedom, love . . .

This, it seems to me, is what it means to truly be holy witnesses to the word and the silence of God, fully engaged in the holy war.

You are already overcomers

The combat we experience on a world encompassing scale is in fact cosmic! It takes place wherever we find the adversary, so its scale is titanesque.[16] However, this is no reason to let our hands fall; the apostle John tells us in his letter, "You have overcome" (1 John 2:13, 14). This is a cause for real amazement. John is not making a promise of victory or an invitation to be victorious. No indeed! He states that we are already overcomers: "You have overcome the Evil One!" How can this be?

The people John was writing to were unaware of their victory, just as we too may be unaware. What does he mean? John addresses his readers as "little children," underlining how fragile they are, how inexperienced, but also how hot headed, headstrong — as children often are.

16. The Greek "titans" were their primordial "gods." (Trans.)

The phrase "little child' chosen here by John is a slightly sly sort of reference. It is taken from the book of Samuel, where it is employed of the youthful David as he prepared to go into battle with Goliath. Seeing this diminutive but intrepid "child" compared to the arrogant enemy, Saul says to his chief of staff, "Abner, of whom is this young child a son?" (1 Sam 17:55). (By way of reply Saul is told, "I don't know; find out for yourself!")

Here in David we find a model for a disciple, a David who is questioned to his face, whom the enemy regards with disdain, but who advances in total confidence in the one who gives him the victory.

Who was it that vanquished Goliath? If David were to be asked he would certainly reply that "God defeated him." Humbly, David honors his God. If we were to ask God, there is a strong possibility he would reply, "No, no; the victory is David's!" Thus the humble God honors his child!

When John tells us, "You have overcome," he is the spokesperson for what God humbly says about us; our place is to also hear what we should be saying: "God himself has won and given us the victory."

"I have overcome," Jesus says; "You have overcome," says John. It is the same verb and the same tense. The disciple's victory is Christ's victory in which we participate and are its beneficiary. This is why even before going into battle, the disciple is already a victor, just like David advancing on Goliath.

The disciple is already a victor, not simply because 2000 years ago Christ won the victory, but also because Christ lives in us, just as stated by saint John: "He who is in you is greater than he who is in the world" (1 John 4:4).

And we know that when the Son comes to take up residence, the Father and the Spirit also come to dwell within.

The holy war is won by the Son; it is conducted by the Father who sanctifies by the Spirit. Victory has its foundation in the unity of the Trinity, a unity which Satan as the one who divides is unable to damage. When, in his priestly prayer, Christ also asks for the unity of the disciples, this is because of the power of unity against this divider. He requests this unity of his Father, not as a recompense for the war but as the prelude to the combat. That they may be one as we are one; then they will be able to fight against the enemy. That they may be one in us, that they may in this way already be conquerors.

In the same way that unity is not a recompense but the prelude to the battle, holiness is not a recompense granted a few worthy Christians but the preliminary endowment given to each one before launching into warfare.

At peace in the midst of war

By way of conclusion to this chapter, I would like to draw your attention to an audacious paradox which Jesus proposes to us before sending us into the world. The paradox appears in the final verse preceding the priestly prayer. It is clearer if we translate the Greek word for word:

> "I am telling you this so that in me . . . you might have peace,
> . . . in the world you will have oppression."

The peace Jesus speaks of is not the peace that follows war but a peace which he already gives us beforehand by the hearing of his word, so that we might have within us this peace at the very heart of the oppression. The saint

75

already knows this peace right in the midst of the struggle since we has been brought to peace by the word. The saint is at peace during the war; we fight at peace. It is a paradox which in God is the word of truth.

If the saint is at peace on the battlefield it is because we know that the battlefield is in the first place a sanctuary. The paradox Jesus enunciates is doubly tied to our mission into the world; in the world the disciple is at peace as in the peace of a holy place; we are also at peace in the midst of the oppression of a battlefield. If the peace is unbroken, even at the heart of the war, it is because the war is provisional, temporary, while the liturgy, the cosmic worship is unceasing, eternal.

The contemplative gaze fixed on the world is not a romantic gaze which sweetens reality and only sees what is beautiful. It is a look of love which loves unfailingly since it knows the suffering world in which victims and torturers alike are wounded beings. Contemplative love is compassionate love which weeps over the suffering of the world and also weeps for joy at the victory of Christ. The tears of the contemplative mingle with prayer in the sanctuary that is the world.

4

THE BATTLEFIELD OF THE HUMAN HEART

JUST AS THE WHOLE COSMOS IS A TEMPLE, THE HUMAN heart is one too; human praise reaches its fullness when it resounds through both the sanctuary of our own inner being and the sanctuary that is the cosmos. Only then is humanity truly human, in the image of God at the heart of creation; not only heaven and earth, but the person too in his or her entirety is filled with the glory of God.

In the same way, where the external cosmos has become a battlefield, the human heart has too, and the holy war that unfolds before our eyes in the world also unfolds in our heart. This is a spiritual reality of which we became painfully aware the day we realize that the adverse powers that are at work in the world are also at work in our heart; how true it is that we are subject to a twofold assault, externally and internally. It is a tough reality to accept, but our hearts too are a battlefield!

If the disciple's heart is a battlefield, it is because it is shared between two masters. We wish to obey God, but we also find ourselves responsive to the solicitations of the prince of the world; and we obey him. It's simply the case that the disciple' heart is in a tug of war, shared, divided between God and the enemy, between truth and lies, light and darkness.

Prayer for internal unity

Jesus knew what was in man (John 2:25); he knows the disciple is pulled in two directions; this is why he prays with insistence that his disciples not only be kept from the Evil One and sanctified, but also that they may be unified within themselves, internally: "Father, may they all be one, just as we are one."

Jesus is so exercised about the interior unity of the disciples that this is apparent at the very outset of his requests to his Father. In fact his first petition concerning the disciples is this in verse 11, "Holy Father, keep them . . ." and this petition is expanded in a phrase which reveals Jesus' major concern: "Keep them that they may be one." The interior unity of the disciples is therefore Jesus' main preoccupation for them. It is so important to him that he comes back to it, insistently, at the close of his prayer: "May they all be one as you, Father, you are in me and I am in you, that they also may be in us . . . I have given them the glory that you have given me, that they may be one as we are one, I in them as you are in me, that they may come into perfect unity" (21–23).

The request for the sanctification of the disciples is inserted between these two pleas (between vv 11 and 21–23) since it is linked to them; there is no unity without holiness.

Internal and communal unity

"That they all may be one": today we read this request of Jesus as a reference to community, and we understand it with regard to different communities concerned for unity: the unity of our parishes must be maintained, the unity of each of our churches, whose fragility we know so well, or the unity of the Church universal which has been so long divided. The ecumenical movement is based on this reading of the high priestly prayer — "that they may be one together."

However, this reading focusing on the communal, which is habitual with us, is relatively recent in Church history; it is important we realize this. The Fathers understood Jesus' petition in quite another sense, understanding that Christ was praying not so much for the unity of the Church but for the internal unity of each disciple. The Fathers saw meaning not as "that they may together be one," but rather "that each of them may be one"; this is an entirely viable and interesting reading of Jesus' prayer; I indeed believe that it is the reading that the Gospel itself most invites, without doing away with the communal aspect.

It is not a question here of opposing these two readings to each other; they complement and enrich each other. The important thing is not to forget another fundamental fact, that the unity of the Church will be perfect when each Christian is unified in him or herself. How else could the unity of the Church be solid if it is founded on people who are divided in themselves? How could God unify the disciples as a group if he does not also unify them in their inner beings?

When the Fathers were so attentive to this inner unity of being, no doubt this is because they were for the most part monks, which is to say, men thoroughly exercised over this search for unity within; this is true to the extent that Dionysius the Areopagite, for example, thought that the word "monk" (*monos*) means "a person who is one." For a monk, the priority with regard to unity is unity of being;

a person who has attained the unity of their heart can work efficaciously for the unity of the Church.

Though we are not monks, we too are confronted by the division of our beings as a reality of our daily lives to a much more immediate degree than by divisions in the Church, so the patristic reading of John 17 is also always pertinent to us.

The division of the human heart in the Gospels

Jesus reckoned firstly not with the division of the disciples as a group, but much more with the divided heart, so his request addressed to the Father seems above all to be directed at the unity of each disciple, with the unity of the Church as a consequence.

Jesus' teaching always points to inner, personal divisions, not divisions within the Church.

Thus, when Jesus tells the parable of the two sons (Matt 21:28–31), he was not intending to emphasize the division between the two, but rather the contradictions within each of them; one of them says that he is going to the vineyard, but doesn't go; the other says he is not going, but goes all the same. Both of them are divided in what they say and what they do, in their speech and their actions. Jesus underlines this as a plea for coherence of being; which he summarizes in a celebrated formulation, "Let your yes be yes, and your no, no" (Matt 5:37, then Jas 5:12).

In just the same way, when Jesus insistently takes on hypocrites, it is always to denounce the scandalous discord between what is in a person's heart and what appears outwardly. Hypocrisy masks a heart of darkness with a show of light.

Jesus also encountered those who courageously dared admit their inner disunity. Thus, for example, the father of a possessed boy who came to Jesus with a wonderfully truthful statement revealing just how torn a heart can be between faith and non-faith: "I believe! Help my unbelief!" (Mark 9:24).

That Peter too was an abode of both faith and doubt is so evident in the way he first walked on the water and then began to sink (Matt 14:29–30). The same Peter on one day confessed Christ (Matt 16:16) and on another denied him (26: 69–74). Jesus revealed the inner conflict of his disciple, telling him first that his thoughts were those of God (Mt 16.17), and then that his thoughts were inspired by Satan (16.23).

As it was with Peter, so it is with us all. This is why Jesus puts us all on our guard against this division of being: "No one can serve two masters . . . You cannot serve God and Mammon" (Matt 6:24).

In short, when Jesus emphasizes the division of self rather than the Church, it is doubtless becomes inner division comes first, and strife among the disciples flows from it, not the other way round. Divisions in the Church are a consequence of strife in the heart.

Patristic exegesis

The Father well understood which division was the primary and this is why they were much more concerned about the unity of the heart, and why they understood Jesus' request for unity as looking firstly towards interior unity: "Father, may they all be one within themselves, each of them, equally."

As an example of this patristic reading, the only commentary of John Cassian on Jesus' request for unity has nothing to do with the unity of the monastic community in which he lived, but rather the unity of each monk, including the solitaries. Thus, he affirms that Christ's prayer will be fulfilled when "God is the whole of our love and desire, our whole study and our whole effort, all of our thought, all of our life, our speech, our breath" (Conference 10.7). Behind this statement we can sense the first commandment, which requires of each of us an undivided love, "With all your heart, with all your soul, with all your strength, with your every thought"; in short, with our whole being perfectly unified.

Another example among so many is this prayer of Guillaume de St Thierry,[17] meditating on the unity of each soul in God: "The soul, by tasting and seeing your delights in the great and ineffable sacrament (the Eucharist), is changed into what it eats, becoming bone of your bone, flesh of your flesh, and so thoroughly that the prayer you made to your Father on the way to your passion, is found to be fulfilled; the Holy Spirit works in us by grace what he is from all eternity in the Father and in you, the Son of the Father; as you are one, so we are one in you" (Meditation 8.5).

The first thing in the spiritual life is unity of being. What good is it to work for the unity of the Church if we fail to work in the first place towards the unity of our own being, when our inner strife contributes toward accentuating the division in the Church? Moreover, it is a real miracle when God achieves any sort of *rapprochement* between Churches when the disciples are so internally divided!

17. Benedictine and Cistercian monk of the 12th century. (Trans.)

Manichean error (2)

The error of Manicheans is to believe that we are completely, wholly, in God's camp facing the enemy, without seeing that a part of ourselves sides with the opposition. Manicheism has a thick skin! Christ is the only person in whom the prince of the world has no part (John 14:30). In each of us, the adversary has a foothold; he has a certain hold on us and has sown his tares. In each of us light and darkness face off, lies and truth.

The Fathers discovered the division of their selves when they went out into the desert as monks, supposing thereby to flee the world and its conflicts, and so find themselves wholly given over to God and to his praise in the sanctuary of the cosmos. Once in the desert, though, they discovered to their surprise that the world was not only at the other end of the desert but also in their own hearts! Truly a painful discovery! Deep in themselves they found both the world and the conflicts they wished to flee!

No doubt you have made the same unhappy discovery, reader friend! Perhaps you have gone on a day's retreat to immerse yourself in God's light? Perhaps you then found just how deeply the darkness of the world you sought to put at a distance was lodged in your heart! O the paradoxical desert, where both the light of God and the darkness of our hearts are revealed!

Also though, thanks to God, the painful realization of the Fathers proved salutary, causing illusions as to our real condition before God to evaporate, stimulating a still deeper seeking that produced fruit which is so greatly beneficial to us today.

When we hear Jesus say in his prayer, "they are in the world" (17:11), we should add humbly, "and the world is in us"!

Jesus never formulated such an addition, and no doubt this is why the Manicheans were so mistaken. So why was Jesus silent on this point? No doubt out of regard for us, out of modesty, so as not to insist on it to our shame, or discourage us in the struggle . . . ! Jesus never explicitly said that the world is in us, but he did leave it clearly understood when he says, for example, that "out of the heart of man issue evil intentions, murders, adulteries, immoralities, sacrilege, false witness, insults" (Matt 15:19).

These words of Jesus were addressed to the Pharisees, so a Manichean might think the heart of the Pharisees was evil but not the heart of the disciples! Similarly, it was to the Jews, not the disciples, that Jesus said, "the Word of the Father has no place in you" (John 5:58), or again, "you have not the love of God in you" (5:42).

If the Word and the love of God are in a disciple's heart, can we not also recognize that there are words there are not God's and other loves besides the love of God? Can we not also recognize that the different thoughts we find in ourselves are conflicting, and that the same is true of the different loves we carry around? While the Manichean may not wish to acknowledge it, I believe that the Christian sooner or later comes to the conclusion of Christ: the heart of a disciple is truly a battlefield!

Manicheans were mistaken as to the real state of the human heart, the fault of not really having listened to Christ's teaching.

The Holy Spirit and sin both dwell in our heart

If the Fathers could see that the heart of disciples is neither truly pure nor innocent it is because they were helped in this by the apostle Paul himself.

With great lucidity and humility, Paul wrote to the Romans about how divided he felt, unable to do what he desired, and doing what he desired not to do! "It is no longer I that do it, but *sin that dwells in me*"! (7:17) He repeats this sorrowful confession: "When I do what I don't wish to do, it is not I who act in this way, but *sin that dwells in me*" (7:20).

Paul is so humble that he speaks only of himself without actively denouncing the same reality in his readers; "in me," he writes, not "in you"! Humbly, Paul does not generalize, but he does enable us to see what is in each of us.

A little further on in the same letter, Paul says something quite different and very positive about his readers; he says not that sin dwells in them but that the Holy Spirit does, firstly in a doubtful way, "if it is true that the Spirit of God dwells in you"(8:9), then completely positively: "the Spirit dwells in you" (8:11).

The wonderful and humble apostle says only of himself what could be applied to all. We marvel to learn, thanks to Paul, that the Spirit of God dwells in us, but we need also to be sufficiently humble to recognize at the same time that sin dwells in us too.

This is the origin of our internal division, this twin residence in our heart, that of sin, unhappily, and then the Spirit, for our salvation.

With regard to this twin presence we need to make an important comment along with the Fathers, one that is a determinant of our spiritual life. If the Holy Spirit and sin both have a place within us, it is clear that of the two it is God who is the legitimate proprietor, so we can properly say that we are his temple, his residence, his property. When it comes to sin, it is only there as a lodger, a squatter, with our more or less tacit agreement; this means that our heart, our inner sanctuary, needs a serious clean out, or even purging, to chase out the encumbering, undesirable tenant, just as the merchants were chased out of the temple.

Even though it is tough for us to live in the fullness of it, God is our one true owner; we are his temple, not sin's! If it were otherwise, we would have reason to despair! However, it is correct to say of us what we have said about the cosmos, that we are, by God's grace and from the very beginning, temples of God; we have also, unfortunately, become houses of trade in which sin is rife, but without ceasing to be temples of God.

The way of repentance

The recognition that the world is in us, and that the prince of this world has his part in us, means stepping onto the way of repentance, and doing so in a very serious way.

It is not enough to separate ourselves from the world; we also need to eliminate the world from within. When the prodigal returned to his father, he may well have left behind the pigs and the prostitutes, but he still bore their fragrance! Once he was in his father's arms, the way he smelled told where he had come from! Indeed, we still bear the scent of all we heartily wish to quit! But there is more to this.

After quitting the prostitutes and the pigs, the prodigal still had his memories and thoughts which he could not be rid of as easily as the scent. A good bath does away with the bad smells, but pardon does not chase away the memory of what was pardoned and which we truly wish to forget. The memory we have of our sin weighs heavily on our behavior even after forgiveness. The memory does, though, serve to keep us on our guard against the things which continue to stalk us. We are forgiven, but the sin is still a threat to us through the memory we have of it, and this helps to make us very prudent with respect to the adversary.

If the memory of a particular sin keeps us somewhat circumspect, then the memory of habitual sin more strongly claims our attention. The more habitual a sin becomes, the greater is our fragility, our vulnerability, and so much the greater should be our attachment to God, since at any moment the struggle might return.

"O God, create in me a clean heart" (Ps 51:12). This indeed is what we need to be saying to God and to expect from him. When it has once been resident in us, sin leaves behind its marks, its memories, its scent . . . God must not only chase out the intruder but also regenerate the heart from top to bottom; he has to create anew, and only he can do it; our place is to abandon ourselves to him.

We are no longer one

To speak of us as divided is not an ontological statement about the nature of creation; more precisely, it is a recognition of what we have become, a clinical statement about a profoundly diseased state present in humanity, but not one that constitutes our essence. We did not issue from God's hands divided. We were created one, in the image of the one God. The creation meant merely being exposed to the possibility, susceptible of being divided, but not in a fatal way.

Had we left God's hands divided, our state would be without hope, but the Bible says nothing of the sort, and this invites us to constantly turn towards God full of hope.

The same is true of the Church; it emerged from God's heart as one, undivided. It may have become divided, but in God is still one; this should surely enliven our hopes.

If we are divided it is not God's fault but ours, individually and collectively; on the one hand because we allow the "divider" (the meaning of the word "devil"[18]) to be at work within us; and on the other because we are instinct with a humanity which collectively allows the devil access. We are all personally and collectively responsible for this state of affairs. The Christian is no exception, despite anything Manicheans might think.

Perhaps, though, I am mistaken about you, reader friend? Perhaps there is no division in you? Perhaps you are an exception? In that case, forgive me, close this book, but don't forget to pray for me . . . !

Some biblical examples

The Bible speaks about the division in humanity in a very clear way, with no suggestion that it is something that concerns only pagans, and certainly not that we issued from God's hands in this divided state.

Psalm 12 speaks of duplicity of heart in very plain terms; taking the passage word by word there can be no mistake about this — the "double heart" in the Hebrew is "one heart and one heart"(12:3)! A statement like this could not be an ontological (literal) truth!

Having a double heart means having two discursive activities going on at once; that is, to be saying one thing but thinking another, speaking well but thinking ill, to speak the truth when there is deceit within. It also means having two divided affections, the love of God and its

18. *Diabolos* in Greek.

contrary; it means being torn between the two. With a great deal of both wisdom and realism the Bible tells us that "the double-hearted man is not to go to war" (1 Chron 12:33), perhaps because such a man is bold in his speech but timid in his actions, or perhaps, as the Septuagint understood it, because he has acquaintances in the other camp. He is "*eteroklinos,*" the Greek says, with a leaning towards the other side!

James (1.8) speaks of the "double-souled"[19] or "divided soul," which again is not an ontological reality! Such a person is specified by the apostle to be "inconstant in his behavior" since he is torn between two wills, two desires, or two loves. The way the apostle speaks to people like this a little further on (4:8) shows that he is not talking about pagans, but quite simply about Christians who love both the world and God (4:4).

How true it is that we love both God and our adversary, that we have within us both the desire for God and for multiple "things we have not," the desire for power, for money, for pleasures, for human glory . . . all this in such a way that our soul is deeply divided and our heart truly a battlefield.

Paul writes to Timothy: "let the deacons not be of two words."[20] This too is an aspect of our divided being, and not among pagans but Christians since the concern here is deacons. If deacons are officiating in public worship and pronouncing liturgical prayers which are contrary to the thoughts of their heart, it would be better for them not to be deacons. If the deacons are ones who are involved

19. The usual English version is "double-minded"; the Greek is *dipsuchos*, which is closer to two souled. (Trans.)

20. Again, this is closer to the Greek than our traditional "double-tongued." (Trans.)

in service to the poor but their charitable words are not matched by their thoughts, again it is preferable that they not be deacons since hypocritical love does more harm than good.

All these biblical passages show that the division of being is not ontological but of the nature of a disease, a malady the only relief for which comes from God's medicine chest, from God, who alone can treat and heal.

The struggle with thoughts

The biblical texts also indicate that the unhealthy divisions of being always affect the way we speak and even the "self-talk" of our thoughts. It is deep down, at heart level, that each person needs to be cared for, and this means at the level of our thoughts. The care, the help apportioned by God require as our part that we fight — with God's help. The struggle with evil or impassioned thoughts is the inner struggle on the great battlefield within each of us.

Those internal words of our thoughts and the word of God dwelling within us, these together constitute the inner conflict.

We see how this pulls together everything we have said previously about the holy war, except that now the war is not external to us but internal.

The thoughts were what so drew the attention of the Fathers, desirous as they were to be led by the word of God alone. All their efforts consisted firstly in discerning, with God's help, which of their thoughts were wrong, opposed to God, and then warring against them, to chase them away and to give God back his due place, that is, occupying every last inch of territory.

The holy war is the war between the word of truth and the evil thoughts which have their source in the father of lies. It is interesting to see how after the denunciation of the double heart, Psalm 12 then magnifies the word of God: "the words of the Lord are pure words, silver tried in the fire, refined seven times" (12:7). This is the word that sanctifies.

Judas divided

The exemplar of the divided person in the Bible is undoubtedly Judas. This disciple was truly attached to Jesus, and the kiss he gave him was surely not simply hypocrisy or just a sign to the soldiers as to who to arrest. "Rabbi!" this word also expresses Judas' attachment to the Master. Yet Judas had other ideas too, ideas which led him to accept the price of betrayal. He is revealed as being attached to money. The remorse which then filled him shows that there was an intense internal conflict between the two pulls, his love of Christ and his love of money. This inner struggle saw him lean first towards love of money and then towards the love of Jesus, which he manifests by returning to the Temple and flinging down the blood money (27:5). By going to the Temple, he was looking first to God for support; but God's representatives told him that he was searching in vain for help from that quarter: "What is that to us! See to it yourself!" Then, believing himself abandoned by God and no longer able to fight on alone, Judas finished things by killing himself. His death shows how very divided he was: "He burst open and his guts spilled out" (Acts 1:18). He died, split down the middle.

God alone unifies

Who is able to heal such a sickness in our very being? Or, to stay with the vocabulary of warfare, who can enable us to bring an end to our inner conflicts? God alone, surely, as the case of Judas demonstrates. Without God, no internal conflict has any resolution; this is why Jesus asks of God unity for the disciples. It is not that he asks the disciple to be one, but he asks it of God: "Father, may they be one as we are one."

Only God can unify since he himself is one, as stressed in Deuteronomy: "Hear O Israel, the Lord your God is one" (6:4).

Not only is the Father one, but the Son is too, the one in whom the prince of this world has nothing (John 14:30). It is this communion in unity which Jesus speaks of in the priestly prayer: "We are one . . . may they be one as we are one." What a blessing to know that in our inner conflicts we are being borne up by this prayer, the fulfillment of which is in the hands of God, and that, out of love, the Father will fulfill the request of his Son!

When David became aware of the divided nature of his heart and his inability to remedy it, it was to God that he turned, asking him to do what he alone was capable of: "Unite my heart" (Ps 86:11). It is interesting to note that, in this plea, the word for heart is written with a doubling of the final consonant (*levav*), whereas it can be written without this addition (*lev*). According to the exegetical tradition of the rabbis, by speaking of his heart in this way, David was discreetly admitting his duplicity, his internal division.

"That they may be one in us" (17:21)

As he asks his Father for the inner unity of each disciple, Jesus adds a further essential specific, that they may be one "in us."

This is a real revelation: no one can be one in him or herself, independently of God, without God, and it is the tragedy of the non-believer to suppose, first of all that they can arrive alone at a unity of being, but also that the unity lies in themselves. No! As the image of God, we do not have our unity in and of ourselves, but in God, whose image we are. In ourselves we can never be one. We cannot be one except in God, which is to say, more precisely, in the God who is Father, Son and Holy Spirit! What a mystery there is here! God is one because he is triune! The secret of our unity lies in the Trinity! What can we say of this mystery?

"One" means "one in a communion of love"; with this, all becomes clear. God is one because he is a communion of love. He is one but not alone; he is Father, Son and Holy Spirit, a communion of love among three persons. The Father is one because he is in communion with the Son and the Spirit; the Son is one because he is in communion with the Father and the Spirit; and the Spirit is one because he is in communion with the Father and the Son. The unity lies in the communion of love; it is a gift of love which is received in the gift itself. If we are one it is in God that we are one, in this communion of love which causes us to be in God and God in us, as the Father is in the Son and the Son in the Father. It is in this communion with God that we find communion with others and so our unity with others.

Without God, we cannot be unified; we isolate and cut ourselves off from the source of love which alone is able to unify; we are not one, just isolated!

Jesus was never isolated; by contrast, it is said that he was "alone" (Matt 17.8 . . .).[21] When it says that Jesus was alone, it means that he was in God, one (alone) in God.

When a monk seeks solitude it is to be in God, and if not, he is mistaken. He seeks his unity in God, and it as he receives this unity that he finds himself in communion with all else. As Evagrius magnificently says, a monk is "separated from everything and united to everything."

The struggle for internal unification

Every quest for internal unity is accompanied by a struggle with the "divider." It was to prepare the disciples for this struggle that Jesus asks his Father to sanctify them, thereby making the struggle a holy war. The internal struggle for unification of being is a holy war, which is to say, a war conducted by God against adverse powers which seek to divide the self and separate it from God and others, and so dominate it. It is a war in which we are called upon to give the best of ourselves, always relying entirely on God. The true holy war is just that, the interior war which unfolds on or in the battlefield of the human heart.

The image of David and Goliath comes to mind once more. Our enemy, indeed, is a veritable giant against whom we can do nothing if we fail to place our total trust in God. David fought out of love for God and his people. God was mysteriously engaged alongside him, also out of love for him and his people. Victory depended on the love

21. The French is *seul*, which has the idea of being one. (Trans.)

communion between God and David. Without love, the holy war is in vain.

It's perhaps in the Book of Psalms that the holy war finds its most beautiful expression. The Psalms, in fact, are given us as an enablement to speak out to God all that we go through in our inner conflicts. They free us in our speech and turn us to God. They also help us understand our experience in these conflicts, which, without them, would remain obscure. Without prayer, the holy war is in vain.

"Sanctify them," Jesus asks of his Father, before sending his disciples into the world which thereby becomes really a battlefield for them. Sanctified for battle, the disciple is therefore called upon to fight in holiness, a holiness received from God, and then growing, until his or her entire being is in God, in communion with him, and so one in God, brought to rest in God, with that peace the world cannot give. In this peace, the disciple continues to fight until their final breath.

In a spirit of love

To go off to a holy war implies a strong attachment to God as well as considerable renunciation. In the Old Testament, someone who went to war had to leave his wife and children, his family and all his goods, for the duration of the war; he had to observe chastity while retaining his love for family and live in poverty in so far as he was to receive his daily bread like manna in the desert; finally his was to be a total obedience to God since the outcome of the war depended on this. Chastity, poverty and obedience always go along with the interior battle, so that each combatant in a way is found to be, in their inner being, a "monk," that is "one," according to Dionysius' thought.

Any battle implies the need for great discipline, a high degree of asceticism,[22] if victory is to be attained. Ascetic discipline is not an end in itself but an aid to spiritual struggle. It keeps the warrior alert; it enables us to give of our best without ever becoming discouraged.

The whole battle is waged in unceasing proximity to God, in total communion with him, a profound communion of love, love being the master word in this war. To love God is to be in him, and is to fight against every contrary affection which attempts like a parasite to lodge in our hearts. The spirit[23] of the struggle is a spirit of love. Ascetic discipline[24] is the necessary effort to keeping this passion of love alive.

With the help of the Holy Spirit

All that we have said about the battle in the world is to be reapplied to the interior battle; that is, the lie is not now seen in others but in ourselves, in the internal, false words of our thoughts. The issue is how to combat false thoughts, thoughts that condemn, that slander, that despise and reject, adulterous thoughts, thoughts that are prideful, jealous, thoughts that . . . the list is a long one! The Fathers compiled a register of hundreds!

Every holy war essentially begins within us. If I fail to fight the lie in me, there is no point in my going to fight the lie in others on the great battlefield of the world. There are more "beams" in me than "specks of dust" in others!

22. DB's book entitled, translating the French, "Asceticism, the way to freedom," discusses this issue at length; it's clear throughout this book that, to the author, asceticism means simply discipline, and that indeed any act of obedience to God is an ascetic act. (Trans.)

23. The French here is élan, which says more than any one word in English: a passion, a movement, a surge, a spirit . . . (Trans.)

24. DB's intent only secondarily suggests physical rigors. (Trans.)

The first task, before any combat, is to discern between the truthful and false thoughts, between the thoughts of light and those of darkness. There is no such discernment possible without the Holy Spirit.

When the tempter falsifies the word of God to recruit and use it against us, we are unable to discern this without the Holy Spirit. Without him, we fall into the tempter's traps. This is just what happens! Some word or other of God's comes to mind and we use it falsely to clear ourselves! We can justify this or that poor behavior with the word of God and think we are doing well! We have to deal with traps of the devil that we do not always see. Once again, only the Holy Spirit can bring light. Without him we can do nothing.

With the Spirit's help we can also discern in our hearts between God's peace and the peace of the world so that we can combat the worldly peace in its falsity.

With the Spirit's help we can discern between the joy of God and worldly joy; and combat the latter.

With the Spirit's help again we can discern in ourselves the violence of God, that holy violence which opens the way into the Kingdom of God and which Christ knew when he chased the merchants out of the Temple, and the worldly violence which is a bearer of death, not purification.

The holy war can assuredly in no way be fought without the help of the Holy Spirit. Jesus himself departed for the desert to battle the tempter with the Holy Spirit (Luke 4:1). It should be the same for us in each of our struggles. Our very first act must be to implore him, "O heavenly King, comforter, Spirit of truth, you who are present everywhere and who guide all things, treasure of all goodness and giver of life, come and live within us; purify us of all that defiles, and save us, O you who are kind."

Humbly

The inner struggle, as with any struggle, involves hardship, since it is so often made up of defeats and checks. Every setback wounds but it makes us humble too. Each defeat, in the final analysis, is due to our pride, in presuming too much on our own strength and not counting sufficiently on God's; or to our pridefully believing ourselves safe from the assaults of the adversary. Each setback makes us humble before God, but also in our own eyes and those of others, whether or not they witness our defeats. Each setback throws us back on God as humble mendicants within a fellowship of ever increasing love.

The struggle is all the more painful in that God also at times seems to do us ill so we believe that he is fighting against us too! Let us not, however, mistake this. In the inner struggle, God is not fighting against us, but with us. If he acts harshly towards us at times, it is precisely because he is combating what needs to be purified; he is driving out of us what needs to be dealt with. He combats our illicit affections, our love of glory, our love of power, of pleasures, of money . . . And each assault of God against these multiple loves affects us and causes us trouble. However, this is how God does us good! He dislodges from our hearts those things we have no courage to deal with. At times he forces us to renounce things we would not otherwise rid ourselves of. No doubt this is upsetting, but we ought to be thankful — this is how we are purified. When he purifies by fire, it hurts; but it is a healing pain.

Without discouragement

The inner struggle makes us humble, but not discouraged, demobilized or desperate. All discouragement, all despair is to be considered a trap of the enemy, since by attacking our hope in God, the adversary distances us from God. We cannot be discouraged if we bear in mind that we are unceasingly being carried by the eternal prayer of Christ: "Holy Father, keep them, that they may be one as we are one." Jesus is not demobilized; he is not discouraged in his intercession for us. The Father does not let his Son's prayer go unanswered and never ceases to sanctify us through the power of the Spirit. If we become discouraged because of our defeats, God is not discouraged from sanctifying us, just as the Son does not become discouraged as he bears us up in prayer, and as the Spirit is not discouraged from abiding in us to help us chase out every undesirable tenant.

If we seem to go from one defeat to the next, we can also recognize that we are proceeding each time to a fresh beginning!

"Abba Moses asked Abba Sylvain, 'Can a man start all over again each day?' The old man replied, 'Anyone who is traveling has to begin again every moment'" (Sentence 866).

Do not lose courage, reader friend! God is not discouraged by our setbacks! We must never lose our thirst for holiness and inner unity! Christ himself thirsts for our holiness and unity, which is why he asks them of his Father insistently. May his thirst make us as thirsty as him!

EPILOGUE

THREE DAYS AFTER THEY HEARD THE HIGH PRIESTLY prayer, the disciples were together, shut up in a house in Jerusalem where they had sought refuge. They had bolted the doors; they were scared. In the meantime, Christ had died. The cross, still standing not so very far away, plainly told them that the world is a battlefield. The Crucified attested this fact, the first victim. The disciples were afraid.

They had still more cause for fear when they considered their own great weakness. Judas had betrayed him; Peter denied him; all had abandoned the Master. Wishing to save their own skin at the heart of the storm, they found that the storm had invaded their hearts. The disciples were afraid, discovering in themselves a real battlefield.

Then it was that the Resurrected One came into their midst. All the doors were still bolted, including those of their hearts, but he was there, in their midst. He showed them the marks in his hands and his pierced side. He was alive! His first words brought to their hearts the very thing they announced, "Peace be with you." Peace drove out the fear and invaded their hearts. The disciples were full of joy. The Son of God was there; his presence made the house a sanctuary, a holy place.

"Peace be with you," he repeated. "As the Father sent me, so I am sending you." Having said this, he breathed on them and said, "Receive the Holy Spirit" (John 20:21–22). In breathing on them, Jesus followed the action of the creator who breathed on his creatures (Gen 2:7) to make them creatures of praise in the sanctuary that is the world. The Spirit of God who hovers over the waters now filled the hearts of the disciples, birthing them into prayer. With him, they could appropriate the high priestly prayer: "Father the hour is come! Glorify your Son that your Son may glorify you, according as you have given him power over all flesh that he may give eternal life to all those you have given him. This is eternal life, that they may know you, the only true God and the one you have sent, Jesus Christ."

Reader friend, Jesus comes to breathe on you and give you his peace. Perhaps you have bolted your door to make a retreat as you read this short book? The world is now open before you and Christ is sending you. He has breathed upon you and given you the gift of the Holy Spirit. Be silent for a moment and allow the Spirit to accomplish within you his work of peace. Your Father is there in secret and waits in silence. He has blessed and sanctified this day that has no evening or morning. Your Father is there watching you, ready to receive your hymn of adoration.

Before you allow your hymn to rise up in the holy place, be silent once more in the silence of God and incline your ear. The Well-Beloved is there, at the right hand of the Father; he whispers as he leans on his breast, "Father, I have given them your word and the world has hated them because they are not of the world as I am not of the world. I am not asking that you take them out of the world, but that you keep them from the Evil One. They are not of the world even as I am not of the world. Sanctify them by the truth; your word is truth. As you sent me into the world, so I am sending them into the world . . . May the love with which you have loved me be in them and may I be in them."

Reader friend, what you hear, there in the sanctuary of your heart, you will also hear when in the world; then your hymn will rise up in the sanctuary that is the world, even as it does in your heart.

Peace be with you!